LIBRARY OF INTRODUCTIONS TO PERSIAN ART

Arthur Upham Pope *Introducing*

Persian Architecture

OXFORD UNIVERSITY PRESS

LONDON

Produced by ASIA INSTITUTE BOOKS
Under the Direction of Jay Gluck

April 21, 1969

Published to commemorate the inauguration of
the ASIA INSTITUTE in the NARENJESTAN, SHIRAZ
Third Impression September 1971
To Commemorate The Twenty-Fifth Centennial
of The Founding of The Persian Empire

DEDICATED TO

HER IMPERIAL MAJESTY EMPRESS FARAH, SHAHBANOU

Patron of The Asia Institute

CONTENTS

SOURCES OF ILLUSTRATIONS

Author 34*t*, 39, 40, 43, 46*l*, 47*r*, 51, 54*t*/*b*, 55, 56, 57*t*, 58, 65*bl*/*br*, 70, 71, 72*bl*/*br*, 76, 77, 78*r*, 81*tl*/*tr*, 84, 85, 87*tl*/*tr*, 88, 91*b*, 92*t*/*b*, 100, 102*b*

A Survey of Persian Art 2*r*, 7*cr*, 8, 12*t*, 13*b*, 14, 17*t*, 21*b*, 29, 30*tr*/*br*, 31(3), 33, 34*br*, 36*bl*, 41, 42*b*, 53, 61, 67, 78*l*, 80*t*, 89, 96, 104, 105, 106, 107, 108*tr*, 113

Asad Behroozan 20, 47*bl*, 57*b*, 64, 65*t*, 68, 69, 72*t*, 79, 80*tl*/*tr*, 86, 87*t*, 90*t*/*b*, 91*t*, 95, 97, 98, 99, 101*bl*/*br*, 102*tl*/*tr*, Corer

Roman Ghirshman 3, 5, 7, 26*tl*/*bl*, 32, 35*t*/*b*

Jay Gluck 9*t*, 21*t*, 24*t*/*b*, 26*br*, 46 *br*, 60, 82-3, 94*t*/*b*, 101*t*, 109, 110*l*/*bl*/*br*, 111*t*, 112, back cover

Other Sources: British Institute of Persian Studies 46*tr*; 47*tl*; Dieulafoy 6; Garson 9*b*; E. Herzfeld 11; Learned Society of Fars 15; S. Lloyd 22; M. Mallowan 2*l*; Ministry of Arts and Culture 19; M. Moghadam 111*b*; R. Naumann 37; Pugachenkova 30*l*; Rostami 12*b*, 13, 16, 17*b*; E. Schroeder (SPA) 53, 54*r*, 108*tl*; USSR 42*t*, 59; M. Wheeler 26*tr*.

THE BEGINNINGS

Architecture in Persia has a continuous history of more than 6,000 years, from at least 5000 B.C. to the present, with characteristic [2] examples distributed over a vast area from Syria to North India and the borders of China, from the Caucasus to Zanzibar. Persian buildings vary from peasant huts, tea houses and garden pavilions to some of the most beautiful and majestic structures the world has ever seen. In meaning and purpose, monumental Persian architecture was primarily religious — at the beginning, magical and invocational in character — by which man was brought into communication and participation with the powers of Heaven.

Available building materials dictated major forms. Clays, readily available at various places, encouraged the development of the primitive *pisé* — molded mud, compressed as solidly as possible and allowed to dry. The abundance of heavy plastic earth, in conjunction with a tenacious gypsum mortar, also facilitated the development of brick. Brick construction lacks the sharp contours, the effects of hardness and weight normal to stone masonry, but on the other hand it permits large, well-defined masses whose broad plain surfaces invite ornamentation that would be inappropriate or even impossible on stone.

For more than 3,000 years, certain design elements of Persian architecture persisted. The most striking were a marked feeling for scale and a discerning use of simple and massive forms, a rather amazing consistency of decorative preferences, the high-arched [84] portal set within a recess, columns with bracket capitals, and recur- [17] rent types of plan and elevation. Some of the earliest styles still survive. The columned porch, or *talar*, revealed in the rock-cut [6,22] tombs near Persepolis; the dome on four arches; the vast ovoid arch [31] of Ctesiphon may still recur in a twentieth century farm building; [34] the four-ivan court, anticipated in Parthian times; earthly towers reaching up toward the sky to mingle with the divine towers of [46] Heaven; the interior court and pool, the angled entrance and exten- [111] sive decoration are ancient but still common features.

Most structures are simple in mass and contour — conveying, from a distance, a spirit of repose and assurance — combined with the controlled excitement that is provided by vast areas of richly colored, intricate ornament which invite leisurely exploration. This combination of stimulation and repose is characteristic of the great friezes at Persepolis and the encrustation of superb faience, as at Mashhad, infinitely fascinating and absorbing in detail. A sumptuous and intensely developed surface ornament was an essential, happily renewed with fresh invention in every period.

24
60

In addition to the influence of climate, available material, religious purpose and peripheral cultures, the patron also played a decisive role in the development of architecture. Great monuments were regarded as both the prerogative and duty of the ruler. Darius and Xerxes, Chosroes II, Ghazan Khan, Timur, Mahmud of Ghazna, Shah ʿAbbas, all committed the nation's resources as well as their own talents to building. Their great buildings were personal monuments, demonstrations of power, personality, rivalries, taste and status.

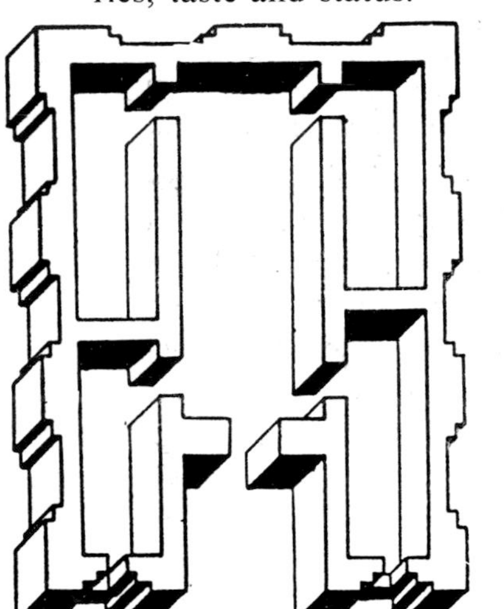

The landscape itself — huge snow-capped mountains, valleys large as provinces, wide shining plains — required constructions conceived and executed in terms of grandeur. In such a setting where ordinary buildings would seem but trifles, a feeling for scale, boldly used, was indispensable. Man was always conscious of his dependence on the powers of that heaven and his chief end was to achieve contact with the ultimate powers, through reverence, obedience and participation and an affirmative architecture.

It was the permanent office of architecture, both physically and symbolically, to bridge the awesome gap between the material world and the heavens by means of structures that reached toward the sky. The symbolic character of the mountain and its crucial role in the maintenance of fertility and life continue throughout the entire history of Persian architecture, sometimes in specific symbols, sometimes in more subtle forms, and commonly in the use of ornament clearly evocative of vegetation.

An important feature of this mountain concept necessarily involves the entrance. Clefts and deep ravines lead into its very heart, and it is through these openings that the god recedes or emerges at the vital moment of renewal. Hence, in early representations of the mountain, the forces of heaven are in contact with the earth. In the earliest temples or ziggurats, which in their form [5] and meaning represent the mountain; this niche, this gate to the divine world, is represented by the great outer portals. They make the first step in the transition from the outer world of fact to the inner world of divine power.

From Zoroastrian times, the beautiful was integrally associated with light. It was an essential component of divine personality.

Opposite:

Tepe Gawra
3200 B.C.

Susa seal, 3rd mill.,
showing houses
or store houses

Rock tomb,
Da U Dukhtar,
Fars

Physical light in Persia — intense, palpable, creative — persuasively expounds the role conferred on it by religion. In Persian art, both lightness and clarity are sought and, conversely, the obscure and confused are avoided.

Love of beauty existed in all classes and we find the humblest tools executed with an often touching taste. That beauty itself was significant, that it was an essential to be cherished and conserved, that, in truth, beauty was an attribute of the Divine, were universally accepted principles. "God hath planted beauty in our midst like a flag in the city," wrote the 14th-century mystic poet Shabistari.

I. FROM THE EARLIEST CIVILIZATIONS TO THE RISE OF THE ACHAEMENIDS

The name Iran, "Land of the Aryans", derives from the tribes which settled on the Iranian plateau, the site of early highland settlements which date back some 10,000 years. The earliest known populations of this prehistoric Persia were distributed in widely scattered small villages. Relations with the more rapidly developing Mesopotamian plain, though warlike, gradually became more and more fruitful. The religious motives so vital to architecture may have originated on the plateau, then been transmitted to the lowlands where they matured and subsequently returned to the Iranians of the plateau. Out of these processes, content developed and maturity evolved. Farming hamlets — small houses with stone in the foundations, walls, and beaten floors — dating from 8000-6000 B.C., have been disclosed by expeditions of the University of Chicago directed by Professor Braidwood. Although these humble structures are hardly architecture, they were its necessary predecessors.

The earliest known phases of building in Iran are, for the most part, in the western valleys. Early neolithic communities at Ali Kosh, in the Deh Luran Valley, are remains of large houses on a level datable *circa* 6200-5800 B.C. The rooms were quite spacious (10 x 16 feet), built of handmade bricks of local mud cut into approximate rectangles and sun-dried.

Jarmo (*circa* 6500 B.C.), Hasuna (*circa* 6000 B.C.) and Tepe 2 Gawra (*circa* 4500 B.C.) in northeastern Mesopotamia, show a similarity of culture as settled "from a mountainous land to the east," which could only have been Persia.

One of the most interesting structures known in that "moun- 7 tainous land" was at Sialk. The oldest settlement there, from the fifth millenium, evidently consisted only of huts made of tree branches. In the next stage, building began with handmade mud brick: an oval lump of earth shaped by hand and dried in the sun. Even at this stage, thought was given to improving structural tech- 7 nique, for on the edges of these bricks, hollows, made by a thumb-

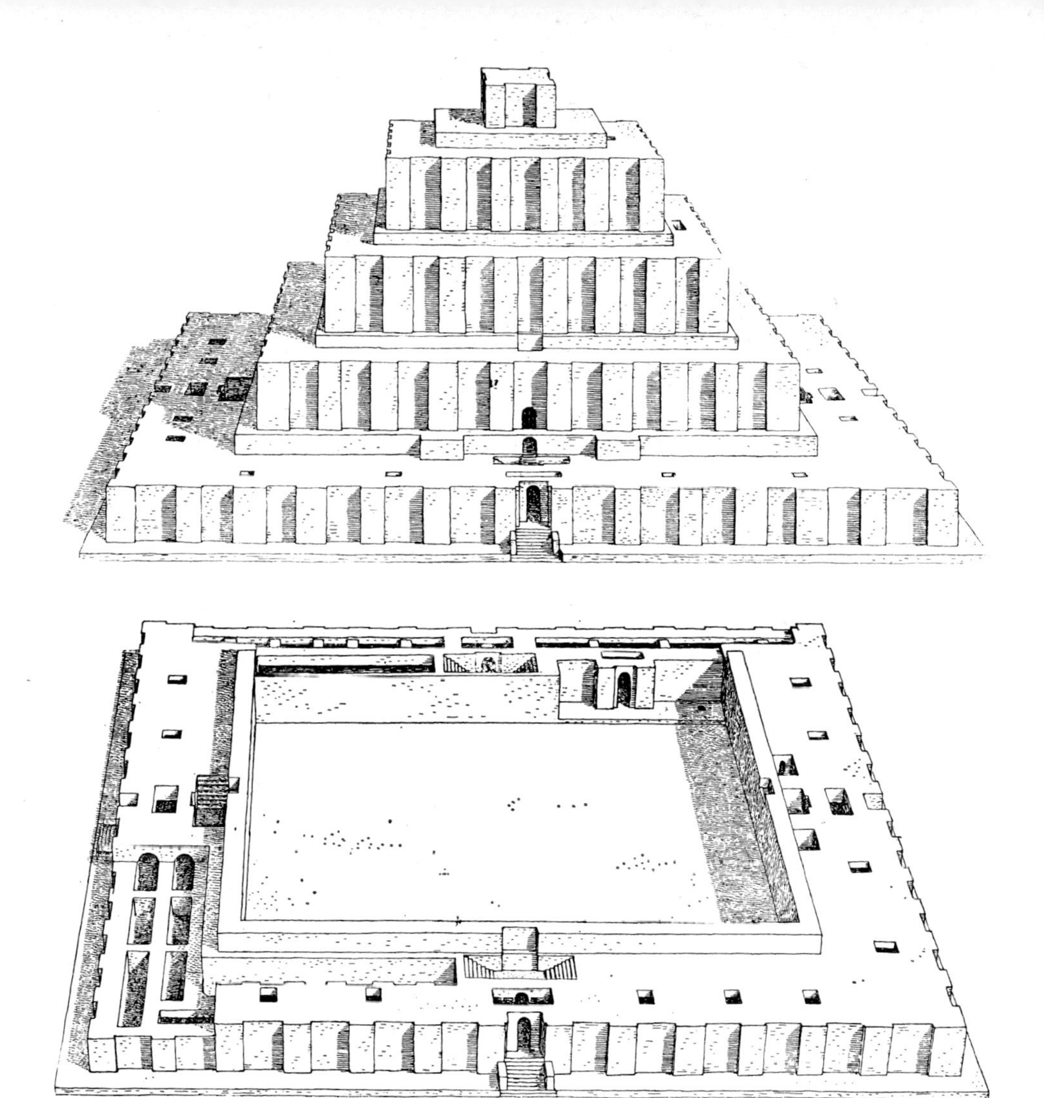

Choga Zambil: below, first structure; above, full ziggurat

print, hold an extra depth of mud mortar. Rudimentary architectural decoration saw the walls of rooms painted red with iron oxide mixed in fruit juice. The modern brick — rectangular, flat-sided, made in a mold — appeared in the fourth millennium, apparently also an Iranian invention.

There existed throughout the ancient Near East a tendency to admire and worship the mountain. Huge ziggurats relieved the flat monotony of the Mesopotamian plain, ritual imitations of the familiar sacred mountains which ring the Iranian plateau. Thus, even if the impressive development of these colossal structures was Mesopotamian (ziggurats were in Sumer by about 2200 B.C.), their inspiration and meaning was clearly Persian. The men who came down from eastern lands could not bring with them their mountains, so they made their own "Holy Hill" or "Mountain of All Lands." Ziggurats came to include all feasible decorative treatments: cone mosaics, colored and glazed bricks.

The Elamites, whose first kingdom dates from the third millennium, provided the link between Iran and Sumer. Perhaps greatest [5] of all ziggurats is the Elamite Choga Zambil. This earliest known Iranian monument of imposing dimensions and character, rivaling the pyramids of Egypt, was built at Dur Untashi, a city

After photo. Pope.

Peasant houses, Mazanderan

near Susa, by Untash-gal, King of Elam, about 1250 B.C. The ziggurat served as both temple and tomb. Composed of five separately built concentric towers of varying heights, the innermost and tallest was 115 feet square at its base and 160 feet high with a complex of chambers, some over 50 feet long, tombs, tunnels, arches, stairways and drains. A temple crowned the flat top. The walls of the ziggurat were extensively faced with glazed kiln-fired brick, blue and green and of a metallic shimmer. Inlaid ivory mosaics were also used and wooden doors were decorated with opaque glass mosaics which depicted prancing animals. Architectural details were rendered in glazed terra cotta.

[14] At Susa, the Elamite capital, three more conventional elaborate palaces can be dated slightly prior to 1000 B.C., although the site [2] goes back to 4000 B.C. Elamite architecture was generally of unfired brick, with red bricks used for revetment. By the twelfth century B.C. glazed bricks were used for decoration, blue and green at Choga Zambil and blue and yellow at Susa. Elamite architecture includes temples built on huge platforms, the interior a square

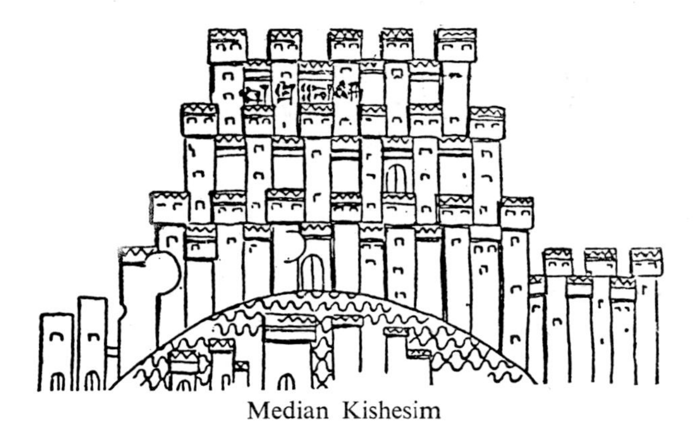

Median Kishesim

Plan of Hasanlu,

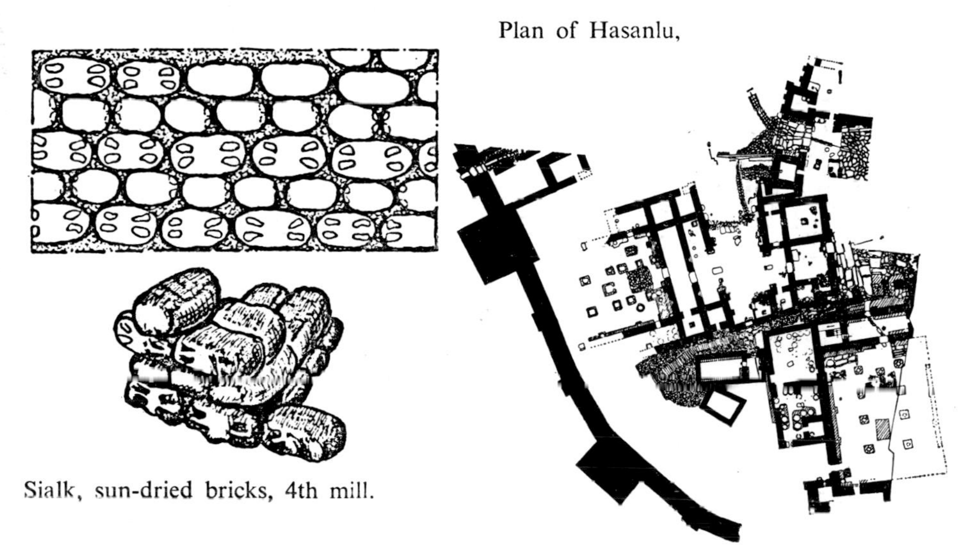

Sialk, sun-dried bricks, 4th mill.

Sialk, tentative restoration

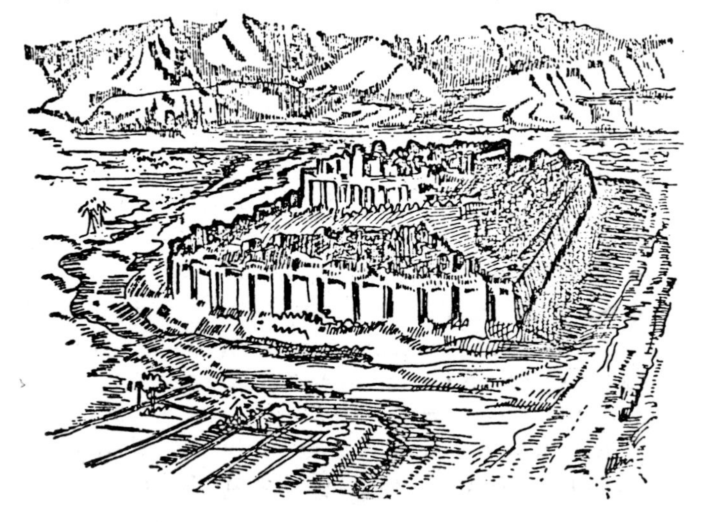

or rectangular sanctuary, sometimes more than one story high, covered with a wooden roof on brick columns. At Susa, some vaults of the Elamite apadana are 16 to 26 feet across.

From about 800 B.C. on the Iranian plateau massive migrations took place. From these the Medes finally emerged dominant. In the late seventh century, their king, Cyaxares, chose Ecbatana (modern Hamadan) as his capital. By the ninth and eighth centuries, in the northwest, an interesting and influential stone and brick archi- 7,8 tecture developed. Assyrian pictorial carvings inform of this

Toprak-Kale, multi-storied building on bronze plaque

Temple of Musasir, Urartu

highly developed architecture. Cities had double, even triple, stone walls 12 feet thick and 40 feet high. The massiveness can be 7 seen in the ninth century fortress of Hasanlu. Buildings seem to have been wooden, square, tower-like structures, with columns which may have been tree trunks. Cyclopaean stone walls topped with high towers had a slight overhang, suggestive of machicolations. Religious buildings, however, were conspicuously different, 8 steeply gabled, with large columns forming a portico, as at Musasir, "almost the exact picture of a Greek temple long before there was anything like it in Greece." (Herzfeld)

Migrant Persian tribes from the north and east settled in the 9 northwest for some time and acquired architectural techniques and a sense of style. These they carried with them to their final home in south Persia, where their influence was seen first at Masjid-i-Suleiman, Pasargad and then Persepolis and Susa.

Traditional nomad tent pitched before Persepolis

The symplegma of the lion slaying the bull:
coat of arms of Persepolis.

II. MAJESTY AND SPLENDOR

THE ACHAEMENIDS
560-330 B.C.

The Persian Empire was established by 560 B.C., when two powerful Aryan states, Media and Persia, were confederated by Cyrus the Great, the first Achaemenid. Because of two extraordinary men, Cyrus, and later Darius I, the whole of Western Asia was organized into the world's first great empire — which lasted for two hundred and thirty years. From the Nile to the Oxus, from the Aegean to the Ganges, a new epoch was initiated, an unaccustomed stability was assured; good government was imposed and a network of efficient communications encouraged commerce and produced immense wealth. The Achaemenid Royal Road from Susa to Sardis covered over 1,600 miles and its one hundred and eleven stations for caravans enabled transportation of goods throughout the empire in less than ninety days; dispatches covered the route in a mere week. The routes from Susa to Persepolis and from Susa to Ecbatana were even paved! All an anticipation of the Roman road.

As the first expression of political power and divine sanction Cyrus began about 550 B.C. construction of the complex of palaces
11 and temples at Pasargad, in the southern province of Fars. A huge
12 artificial platform with enormous stone revetments and the use of tall slender stone or wooden columns recall northern practices.
11 There were three palace buildings, each enclosed by its own large masonry wall. Its size tells the imperial story: the central room of the main audience hall or temple (political and religious functions were intermingled) covered an area 230 by 131 feet (70×30m). Black and white, strikingly combined, as well as rich polychromy (some of the wooden columns were painted blue, green, red and yellow) and impressive use of precious metal plating, all emphasized that this was a city apart, the focus of royal and sacred power. For the holy fire, there was a square tower, now ruined, very like the tower at
13 Naqsh-i-Rustam, a similarity which emphasizes how ancient was the history of the fireworshipping cult.

5 Here, at Pasargad, in a gabled temple recalling early ziggurats
8 and the temple at Musasir, Cyrus the Great was buried. Cyrus'

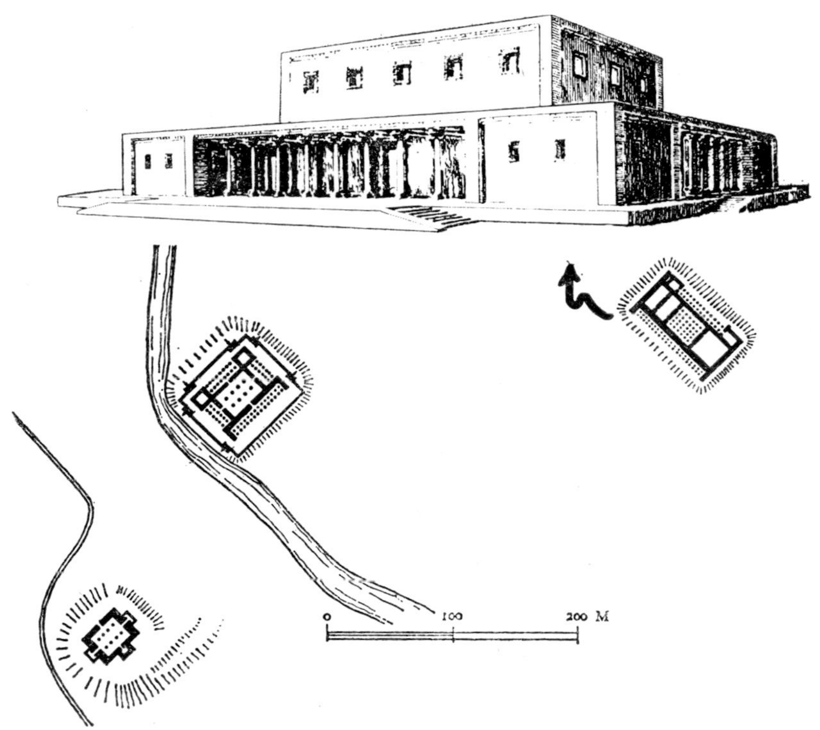

Pasargad, plan with audience hall at center and its reconstruction

temple-tomb crowns six stages which decrease in height as they 13 progress upward, a miniature ziggurat, potent beyond any considerations of dimension. With the exception of this single enduring structure, Pasargad is now largely in ruins, providing little hint of how it must once have appeared. Occupying a beautiful expanse of park-like meadow, it was in fact rather like a nomad camp, its various elements widely scattered. The establishment at Pasargad, imposing though it must have been in many respects, was not adequate as the capital city of a rapidly expanding empire nor as an expression of newly won imperial glory. Cyrus probably selected the Persepolis site before construction was actually undertaken in about 518 B.C., for planning and preliminary work were extensive and difficult. Because Persepolis was the religious capital, it indeed seems logical that a political center would have been conceived at the same time.

By 521, Darius I, having succeeded Cambyses II, decided to build a great working capital at Susa, leaving Persepolis to be de- 14 veloped as a national shrine, as the spiritual focus of the nation rather than its administrative center. It is difficult today to imagine how an imperial capital could have been maintained at Susa, where the heat for seven months of the year is almost insupportable.

Pasargad:
Columns standing at Pasargad

Plan and elevation
Fire temple (?), Naqsh-i-Rustam

Opposite:
Tomb of Cyrus, Pasargad
Plan, showing Islamic columns
Achaemenid tomb, Bospar

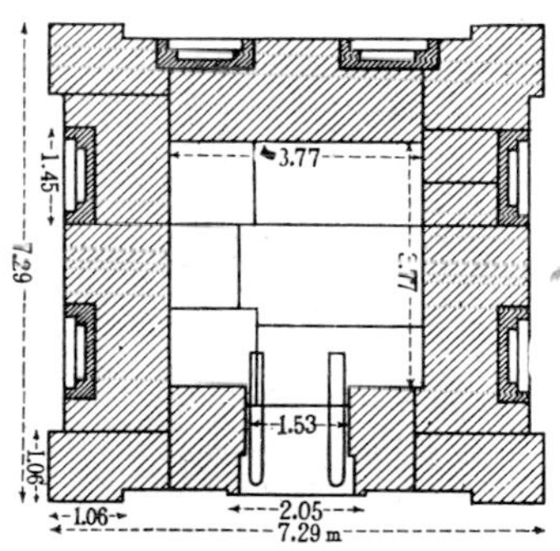
3.77
1.45
7.29
3.77
1.53
1.06
2.05
1.06
7.29 m

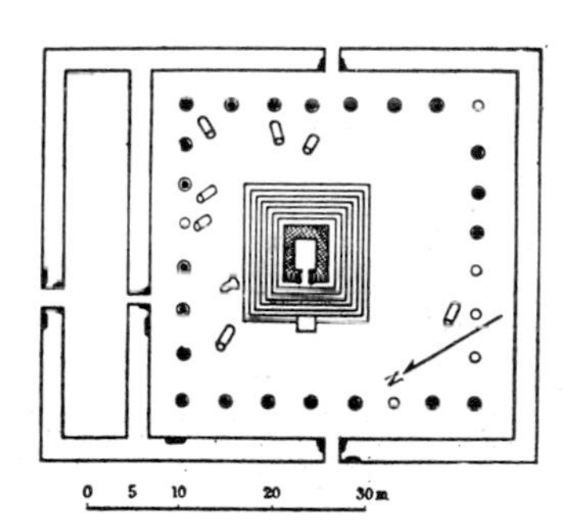
N
0 5 10 20 30m

Dr. Ghirshman, who has spent a great deal of time at Susa in the course of many excavations, states that simply with the introduction of irrigation and the growing of crops permitted by this innovation, the incredible heat has been delayed each year for two or three weeks. Thus, well forested in Achaemenid times, the climate was probably more tolerable. The handsome palace of Darius 14 at Susa is built around a court. An inscription found there gives a remarkable account of its construction. Reading like a builder's contract, it is probably a general guide to constructions at Persepolis and other Achaemenid sites, as well as a propaganda document.

"I constructed this palace. Its decoration was brought from afar . . . The ground was excavated till I came to the firm soil (bed rock) and a (drainage?) ditch was made. Thereupon gravel was

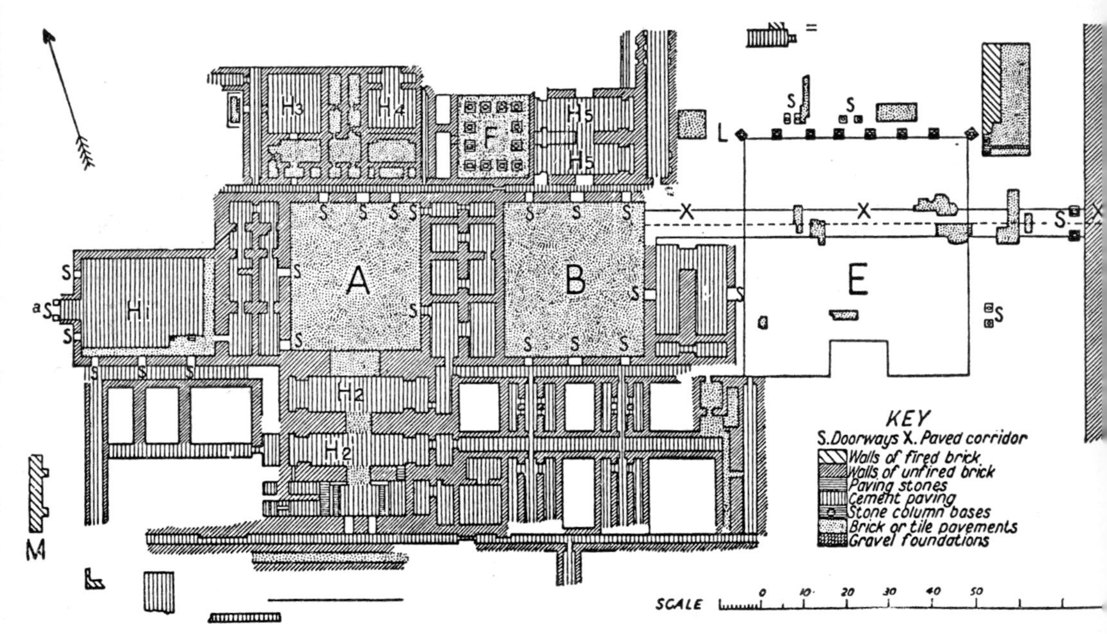

Achaemenid palace, Susa

thrown into it and packed down on one side some forty cubits in height, on the other up to some twenty cubits in height. The palace was erected on this gravel.

"The excavation and the fill and the sun-dried molded bricks were the work of people from Babylonia. The cedar timber was brought from a mountain called Lebanon. The people of Assyria brought it to Babylonia, and the people from Karkha and Ionia brought it from Babylonia to Susa. The wood called *yaka* was brought from Gandhara and Karmana; gold came from Sardes and Bactria and was wrought here. The precious lapis lazuli and carnelian were brought from Soghdiana, and the turquoise from Khwarazm. The silver and ebony came from Egypt. The decoration with which the walls were embellished was brought from Ionia, the ivory from Ethiopia, from India, and from Arachonia, but was wrought here. Stone, here wrought into columns, was from a town called Abiradu in Elam. The stone cutters and sculptors who made them here were Sardians and Ionians. Those who worked in gold were the Medes and the Egyptians. The wood carvers were Sardians and Egyptians. Those who made mosaic in ivory were the Babylonians and the Ionians. Those who decorated the walls were the Medes and the Egyptians.

"By the grace of Ahura Mazda I constructed a magnificent palace in Susa. May Ahura Mazda protect me and my . . . father and my country against injury."

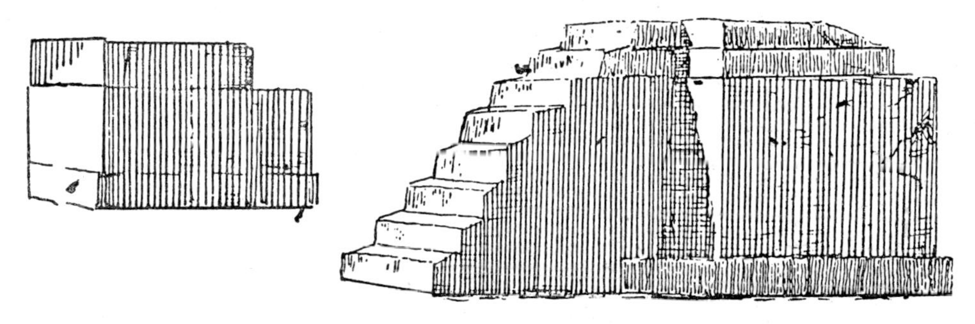

Platforms of fire temple, Pasargad

The first operation obviously was the clearing and building of a great foundation platform, 820 by 490 feet with central court 116 by 118 feet. Paved with brick rubble set in lime and polished with red ochre, this was surrounded by a high, strong wall of unfired brick flanked with projecting towers. Beyond this the river Shavur supplied enough water for a deep moat, which made the slightly elevated site almost impregnable.

Today, Achaemenid Susa is but an instructive ruin, ravaged by its enemies, and destroyed by the Sasanian Shapur II. For centuries local inhabitants have followed the Sasanian precedent, using these older buildings as quarries for new structures. That Susa once contained the magnificent palace of Darius rivaling the splendor of Persepolis, that it was a powerful fort and a flourishing administrative city with a large civilian population, is scarcely evident.

PERSEPOLIS

Apadana columns, Persepolis

16~22 Darius proceeded with the labor of creating a special ritual city: Persepolis. This city, as Darius probably conceived it, would not only glorify the divinely sanctioned dynasty, proclaiming the poli-

Palace of Darius with overlay of column types

tical and religious unity of the state, it would also concentrate and heighten his empire's appeal to the powers of heaven for fertility and abundance, particularly at the great spring festival of the new year. Such a center of terrestrial power, built as an earthly copy of the ancient mythic City of Heaven, would assure concord with the divine. Darius began the great constructions at Persepolis about 518-516 B.C. It was not completed when Alexander destroyed it in 330 B.C.

Apadana and palaces from Gate of All Nations

The unification of political and divine power in the identity of king and high priest, and their affirmation by means of a special architectural ensemble, are as old as Sumer, where Gudea's palace, temple and garden complex were the ultimate antecedents of this Achaemenid sacred city. The imaginary Kangdiz was traditionally described as having seven walls, respectively of gold, silver, steel, bronze, iron, crystal, and lapis. In a long history of symbolic ritual palace-complexes in the ancient Near East, Persepolis was the final and supreme example.

The usual view that Persepolis was primarily a group of impressive palaces built in the capital city of a great empire in order to express political might and to gratify royal pride is Western thinking: factual, literal, rationalistic. It was the dynastic shrine but never, never the political capital: none of the thousands of documents found there are political and the location was quite unsuited for governing an empire. The great kings were in residence only rarely, and temporarily: Susa, Babylon, and Ecbatana, were the seats of government. Persepolis was a sacred national shrine, potent setting for the spring festival, Naw Ruz. By all the resources of symbolic representation, the divine powers were implored to grant fertility and abundance. Persepolis itself exhibits magnitude, power and wealth, with a commanding force sufficient to evoke those powers.

If the Achaemenid kings thus conceived Persepolis as a supreme invocation, the site would naturally be sacred and exclusive. This remarkable creation, one of the wonders of the known world, was unknown in other countries. The Bible, an important source of information on imperial Persian Susa and Ecbatana, has no word about Persepolis. No Babylonian, Assyrian or Phoenician document refers to it. Ctesias, at the Persian court for twenty-four years, has left no mention of it in his history of Persia. Humane sentiments found expression in the nobility and sheer beauty of the building: more rational and gracious than the work of Assyrians or Hittites, more lucid and humane than that of the Egyptians. The beauty of Persepolis is not the accidental counterpart of mere size and costly display; it is the result of beauty being specifically recognized as sovereign value.

Persepolis, backed up against a rugged mountain, commands *19* a wide, mountain-ringed fertile plain. Persepolis was planned as a whole, with complex subsurface systems for water supply and drainage cut out of the solid rock before construction began. A *17* huge platform 900 by 1,500 feet, partly excavated, partly filled, was

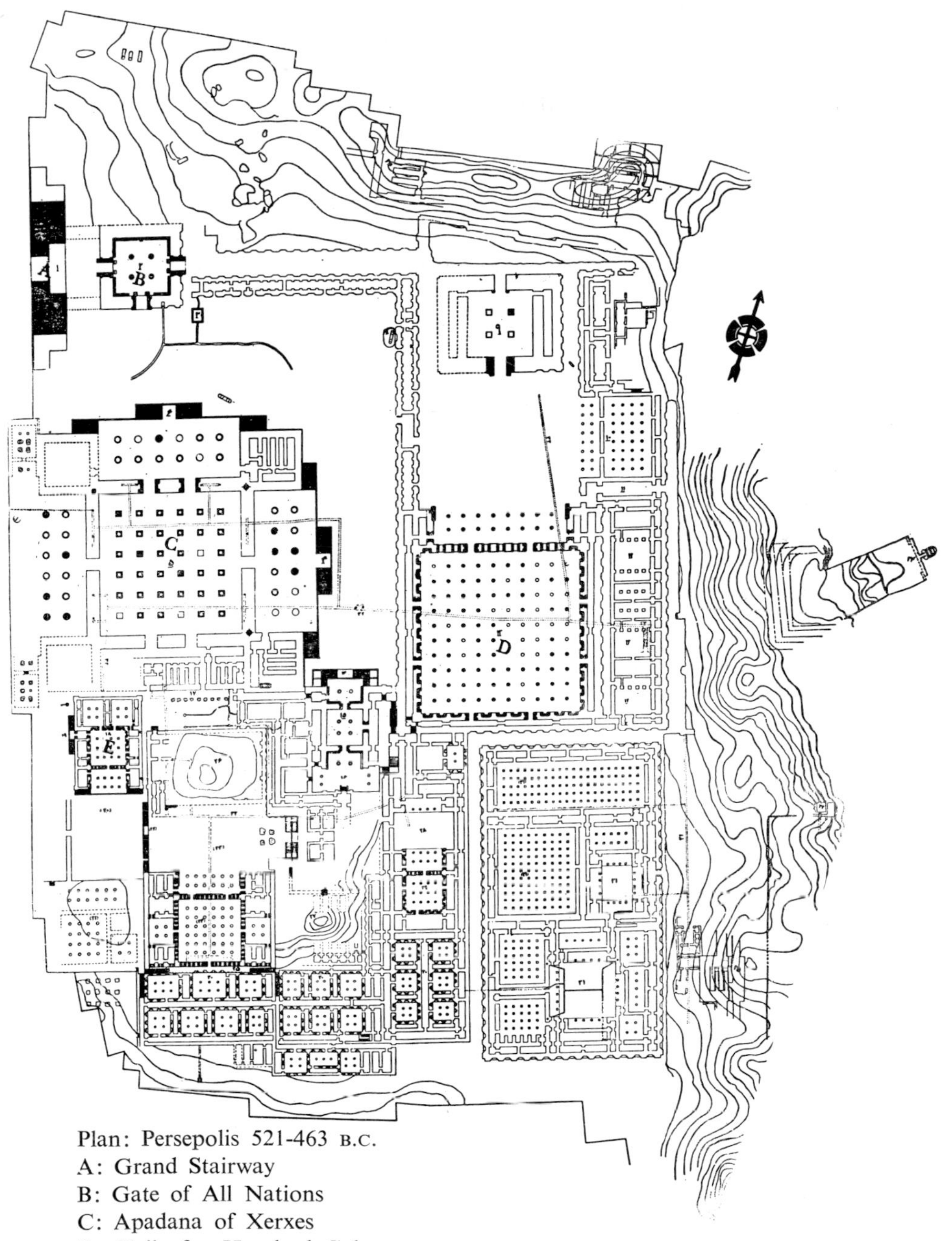

Plan: Persepolis 521-463 B.C.
A: Grand Stairway
B: Gate of All Nations
C: Apadana of Xerxes
D: Hall of a Hundred Columns
E: Palace of Darius

surrounded by a retaining wall, 40 to 60 feet high, made of masonry blocks. Some are 50 feet long and weigh 30 tons, set without mortar and bound with iron clamps. This wall was topped by another of unfired brick, partially faced with polychromed tiles like those at Susa (brown, yellow, green and blue).

The approach itself announced a creation of impressive power: *21* a majestic double stairway 22 feet wide, diverging and returning on *19* itself. These stairs (A on plan), instead of being composed of separate slabs fastened together, were carved from enormous single blocks that sometimes even included a part of the side wall. The grand stairway, of an inclination sufficiently gradual for horsemen, leads to the platform and immediately to a monumental pavilion (B on plan) guarded by colossal human-headed, winged bulls. An *20* inscription by Xerxes proclaims this the "Gate of All Nations". Indeed through this pavilion one entered a world of overwhelming splendor. The high wall excluded the familiar world without, reduced to irrelevance by revelation of sheer grandeur, glowing with color and gleaming with flashing metals.

Gate of All Nations

Apadana and palaces from tomb in Kuh-i-Rahmat

The irregular terrain was built into terraces of various levels so that each structure stood on its own terrace reached by its own monumental stairway. Spaces between buildings formed courts, each with its own garden. Dominating the whole was the Apadana of Xerxes (C on plan), 250 feet square on the exterior, with a central room 195 feet square and porticos on three sides, each 65 feet deep. The whole was sustained by 36 slender columns, elegantly tapered without entasis, 7 feet thick, 60 feet high, and crowned by striking 10-foot bull capitals.

21

17

16

26

Grand Stairway

The interior of the Apadana was a forest of columns, an unearthly vision of the sacred groves of heaven. A reception hall large enough to hold 10,000, it is probable that the processions circulated concentrically toward the king in the center.

Across the court stood the so-called "Hall of a Hundred 22 Columns" (D on plan), probably the rendezvous of the Imperial

Hall of a Hundred Columns, reconstruction

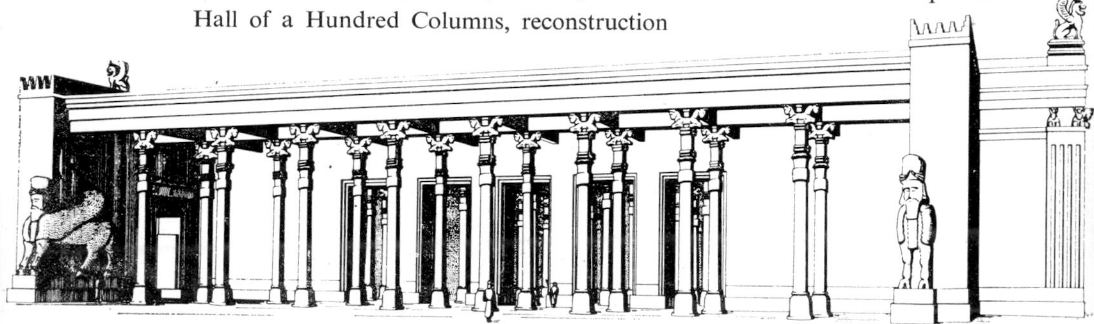

Guard. Beyond the Apadana was the much smaller palace of 21 Darius (E on plan), probably used as temporary quarters during special ceremonies. Here, as in the other palaces, the doorways were crowned with cornices bearing a reed-cavetto pattern, recalling Cambyses' conquest of Egypt. Beyond this lie the palaces of Xerxes and Artaxerxes and other less important palaces and administrative buildings. Outside the walls lay the royal city and the sumptuous palaces and gardens of Cyrus and Darius, for Persepolis itself was occupied by the Achaemenid monarch only for ceremonial, not living, purposes.

The finish throughout the buildings of Persepolis was meticulous, as becomes a royal and sacred building. Some of the walls were polished to mirror brightness and sculptural details often 24 seem to have been executed with jeweller's tools: they are almost as sharp as if cut in metal.

The conception as well as the composition of the sculptural friezes confirms the solemn and humane character of the whole. There is nothing of the violence and agony of Assyrian sculpture; instead there is a lucid and suave simplicity, reserve and tranquillity appropriate to a great, vital moment and to an awareness of a transcendent Presence. Nonetheless, the Persepolis sculptures owe a good deal to Assyrian models and, in some features, to the earlier Hittite reliefs. But in theme, treatment, and mood the differences are profound and instructive. The theme in Assyrian reliefs is the glorification of the monarch, his sanctity, his ruthless and irresistible power, his superhuman achievement in war and his personal prowess in the hunt. The dominant mood was violent and savage.

Actuality was conveyed with force, the spectator, however stirred by the sight, remained passive. The work was done *for* him and not summarized, generalized, nor was it even symbolic. He was left no scope nor opportunity for imaginative supplementation.

Like the Assyrian reliefs the Persepolis friezes are arranged in registers and of shallow relief, but they are of quite a different character. Consistently subordinate to the architecture which they ornament, they are to be seen *en passant,* not leisurely read. They simultaneously embellish and emphasize the structure. Organic to the total mass, limited to crucial areas like portals and foundation courses, their scale and movement is appropriate to the whole. The processions converge on a common point, and their symmetry — divided only by representations of the Tree of Life — provides a gentle rhythm. The Persepolis friezes are united by the forward movement of the procession, by the placement of each figure within the whole group. The spacing is planned, controlled, beautifully but quietly rhythmical. Changes of movement or character within each group subtly alleviate any effect of monotony (except for the long file of the Imperial Guard whose monotony is an evidence of collective and imperial power). The consistent verticals are suggestive of stable support — almost as if they were structural.

Even the huge man-headed bulls that guarded the portals or *20* crowned the columns, formidable and terrifying as they must have seemed, were somewhat humanized by the Persian sculptors. The stance of these monsters at the Gate of All Nations is firm, vital, the huge wings sweeping upward in a fan-like curve, graceful yet alert. By comparison, similar guardians of the Assyrian palaces are heavy of body, relatively inert, wings straight and graceless, expression brutal.

Symbols everywhere confirm the invocational nature of the place. The columns, of which there are five hundred and fifty on the platform, represent the sacred grove, their bases are inverted *26* lotus forms, symbolic of perfection and life-giving power. The capitals of the Apadana porch columns represent the flowering *16* palm with its corona of pendant fronds, while above, vertical Ionic volutes suggest floriation. The bull, a major symbol of primal *26* generative forces here, impregnates the supporting trees which are represented by columns. Thousands of rosette ornaments, tradi- *24* tional sun symbols, acknowledge the sun's necessary life-sustaining force. Even more significant, on the underside of the pivot stones of doors is carved a large open sunflower, placed face down in direct contact with the soil, evidently to transfer directly into the earth its germinating power.

Detail of stairway frieze

9 The symbol of the lion slaying the bull, besides symbolizing the interaction of the two essentials of agriculture, sun and rain, is one of the earliest persisting astronomical myths and perhaps the most important, as Professor Hartner has shown. This fusion of animal forms into a unified symbol, a "symplegma," is found on seals, the earliest of 4000 B.C. and can be traced back further to prehistoric settlers of Persia and Elam. The moment when the constellations Leo and Taurus are at their zenith, coincident with the sun at the same point, coincides with the Spring Equinox, March 21, Naw Ruz, the signal for the Spring plowing. This symplegma has the character of the coat of arms of Persepolis, for it appears in no other Achaemenid monument.

Bull capitals

The row of stepped pyramids that crowns all parapets have 9 been called "crenelations," or "pleasantly ornamental," or even named "battlements," although of no defensive value. They are the repeated symbol of the sacred mountain, used for many centuries on pottery, bronzes, tombs, altars, crowns, painted on doors, and even woven into textiles — everywhere that this sacred and potent form could express a hopeful appeal to the powers of the mountain.

Beyond the deep emotional appeal of these symbols and the assurance of hope and security through magic power — the motive and purpose of this great structure — Persepolis provides magnificence and architectural beauty that are independent of such special purposes. Indeed, it seems independent of time itself.

In regularity and symmetry, Persepolis represents an advance over the relative incoherence of early ritual ensembles. A uniform axis is strictly maintained throughout and even the sculptured friezes are symmetrical. The firm regularity of the plan gives to 19 the ensemble a dignity appropriate to its ceremonial character. The great columns of the Apadana are widely separated (30 feet 16 apart), and gives an unprecedented ratio of voids to solids.

In its true monumentality, larger than any Egyptian temple or medieval cathedral, Persepolis constituted an affirmation of power beyond man. Despite its tremendous size (an area covering 1,300, 19 000 square feet) it was nevertheless unified and consistent, and this was achieved without sacrificing dramatic variety. Although the constructions and carvings at Persepolis were executed over a period of more than a hundred years, one sees very little development or difference in style. The major forms were traditional, restrained by myths whose magic could not be jeopardized by changing the formula, nor by personal preference or experiment. The highly trained designers and craftsmen who produced them must have worked to a strictly controlled plan.

On the same plain as Persepolis, Darius I (d. 486 B.C.) chose the site of his tomb, having it carved out of the solid rock face at 26 Naqsh-i-Rustam. This tomb, clearly modeled on the buildings at Persepolis and Susa, similar to them in its portico, columns, capitals and other details, served as the prototype for later Achaemenid tombs, which were cut into the same rocks. Later, during the Sasanian epoch, when leaders sought to trace their lineage back to the great Achaemenids, this same site of Naqsh-i-Rustam once again became a monument to Persian power.

Opposite

Bull capital, Susa	Capital, Indus Valley
Bull capital, Sidon	
Column base, Susa	Rock-cut tomb, Naqsh-i-Rustam

DIFFUSION

The faltering Achaemenid empire swiftly collapsed under the onslaught of Alexander in 330 B.C. But if Persia as an independent state then briefly ceased to exist, if her political life perished, the vitality of her architectural concepts and superb techniques did not. India, which had enjoyed a sophisticated urban development from the third millennium, eagerly received the creative impulses and skills that came in from the Iranian plateau.

To the native kingdoms of the Ganges valley "Persia transmitted directly or indirectly, not merely the patterns of Empire but important new skills and utilities." By 518 B.C. Darius had conquered and occupied northwest India so that Sind and part of the Punjab — for two hundred years — constituted the twentieth satrapy of the Persian Empire, the largest, most populous and richest of all.

Persian designers, masons and engineers, as well as returning Indians, deprived of opportunities in Persia were eager and well equipped to assist the Mauryan building program. Thus, Megasthenes, only forty or fifty years after the fall of Persepolis, reported that the Indian city Pataliputra outshone even Susa and Persepolis. One hall with eighty columns at Pataliputra and still another mentioned as having a thousand columns were obviously based on the Persian apadanas. Their great stone columns were the first in India and the buildings were set in a large park with trees and fountains, reminiscent of the Persian Paradise Garden. Especially significant is the fact that the columns of these Indian buildings all show the Persian polish, a costly and very slow process, unknown in India before the Mauryan period. One of the remaining stone capitals from Pataliputra is carved in strict Achaemenid style. *26*

Evidence of Persian models and styles in India during the reign of Asoka (264-227 B.C.) is even more varied and abundant: rock-cut edicts, animal capitals (Sarnath, 245 B.C.) and rock-cut and cave temples. The interiors of these rock-cut chambers have the mirror-like Persian stone polish.

This Achaemenid-inspired architecture was modified by local taste and craft habits until, within a few centuries, it was absorbed. In the process, India was substantially enriched and the great Achaemenid tradition grafted onto new roots.

III. IMITATION TO AFFIRMATION

SELEUCIDS—PARTHIANS—SASANIANS: 312 B.C.-642 A.D.

When Alexander left Persepolis in ruins, the spirit of Persian art was by no means totally extinguished. Under the successors of Alexander, Persia's design tradition became temporarily engulfed by Greek importations. After the death of Alexander in 323 B.C., Seleucus, about 312 B.C., took up the reins of the empire. The only Macedonian who had retained his Persian wife, in a limited way he individualized Alexander's vision of a combined Greek and Persian civilization. Hellenic design became dominant but never completely absorbed. Cities were laid out according to geometric Greek plans, temples were built on Greek models and characteristic elements of Greek design were used for ornament. However, acceptance of strongly Hellenic forms seems to have occurred only in areas with concentration of Greek and Macedonian personnel.

Although the ruins of some of these cities have been identified and partly studied, few architectural monuments remain to testify that Seleucid splendor or imagination ever existed. The meager *29* ruins visible today at Kangavar, thought to have been constructed about 200 B.C., show a temple that was quite Greek in character. Only its enormous dimensions, about 66 feet on a side, and its megalithic foundations which echo Achaemenid stone platforms, constitute Persian elements. So little remains of the Seleucid temple at Khurra that it can scarcely be called a monument. Nevertheless, this too was based on Hellenic design.

THE PARTHIANS: 174 B.C. — 224 A.D.

In the northeast of Persia, in what is now Russian Central Asia, another people, the Parthians, were developing a quite different architecture. Combining both Greek and Persian elements, Parthian architecture made singular contributions to the development *105* of architectural form — the achievement of a dome on *104* squinches and the development of the vaulted ivan structure. Unfortunately, few monuments remain standing and the most instructive ruins, except the Rabat-i-Safid, exist not in Persia proper.

Seleucid Kangavar

Although Parthian art is known to have existed from about 250 B.C., it is from 123 B.C. that our knowledge of a widespread Parthian architecture begins. From the ruins of a large palace of the second century A.D. at Hatra, in Iraq, it is possible to see enough standing structure to judge the Parthian capabilities. The main façade, of blocks of masonry, is pierced by two large ivans roofed with high barrel vaults separated by two smaller rooms which were probably two stories high. These later develop into the grand ivan-entrances of the Islamic epoch. Perhaps even more important is the smaller square vaulted chamber directly behind the southern ivan. This subsequently — in Sasanian times and after the Islamic conquest — becomes the square domed chamber so vital to Persian architecture. 29

Hatra, main palace façade, restoration — scheme of roof construction

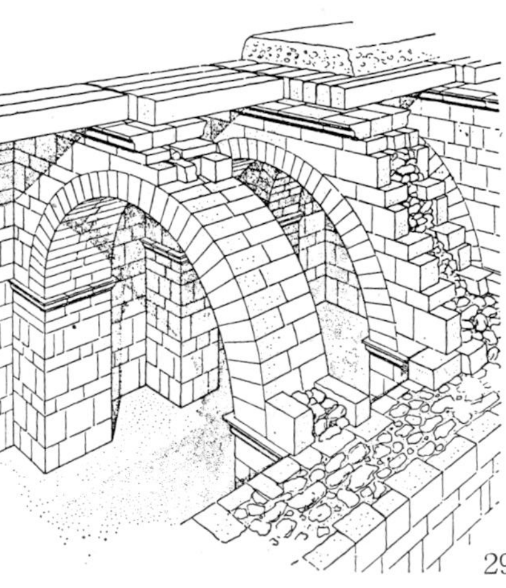

Hatra, mausoleum

Hatra, main palace

Nyasa, Square hall of palace, Turkmenestan 3rd-1st century, B.C.

31 The palace at Ashur, first century A.D. with additions as late as the third century, presents the first known example of four ivans opening onto a central square. This same four-ivan plan becomes basic to Persian mosques, madrassas, and caravanserais.

These major contributions to the development of architectural forms were indigenously Persian, but the Parthian decoration and façade treatment was closely related to Greek themes or, after the successful conquests by Trajan, to Roman forms. The Parthians 31 made widespread use of stucco, both carved and painted, a technique which was to be more fully developed under the Sasanians and later in Islamic Persia.

Ashur, reconstruction

Philostratus described at Palmyra ". . . a room roofed with a sapphire vault, gleaming with heavenly light. Against the blue ground the stones . . . were like stars in the sky. Here sat the King when he meted out justice." And he tells of still another room where ". . . the moon, the sun, stars, and even a portrait of the King shone in a sky of crystal."

Perhaps the earliest example of a domed fire temple dates from the Parthian period. The badly damaged building, a dome on four arches known as the Rabat-i-Safid, crowns a rugged eminence 28 miles southeast of Mashhad.

Neisar

Ashur, reconstruction

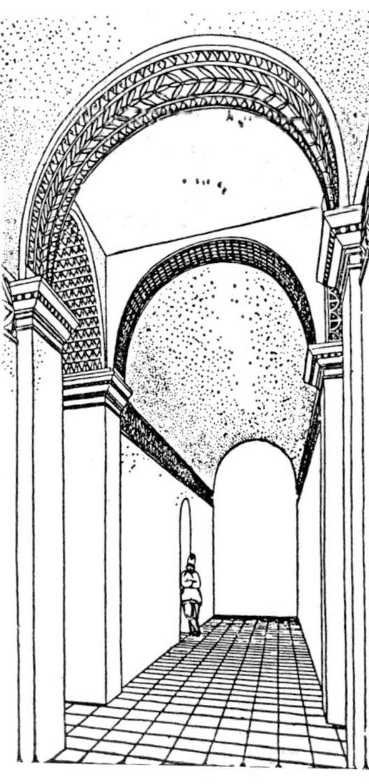

THE SASANIANS: 224-642 A.D.

Ardashir I, the first Sasanian ruler, built his palace at Firuzabad while still a vassal of the Parthian Arsacids. It is, therefore, basically a Parthian structure. This "Ardashir's Glory" was a politically motivated act of rebellion. The palace itself was a remarkable achievement, the focus of a new epoch.

32 The façade was 180 feet long. The vault of the large central ivan spanned 42 feet, fronted by an immense traditional *talar*. Beyond this central ivan, which was flanked to either side by two rectangular ivans, were three square domed chambers supported on walls 13 feet thick.

Patterned on Ardashir's smaller fortified palace, the Kala-i-Dukhtar (a large vaulted ivan, behind which stood a square domed chamber), the later Firuzabad palace was enlarged not only by the

Firuzabad, Ardashir's Glory, reconstruction

ivans, and domed chambers, but by a two-ivan inner court with six small vaulted chambers, doubling the size of the complex.

Of rough-hewn stones set in mortar, the walls of this city palace of Firuzabad were covered with plaster. Decorative detail was borrowed from the Achaemenid palaces at Persepolis. Under the Sasanians the Persian spirit was fully restored to the creative arts.

Sasanian architecture cannot be comprehensively characterized in a single formula. The monuments that have survived — too few — show derivation from heterogeneous sources.

34 The outstanding royal Sasanian monument is the Taq-i-Kisra at Ctesiphon, Iraq. Probably built by Shapur I in the second half of the third century, the remaining section rises above the plain like a gray cliff. Its ivan, a great open vault which spans 75 feet — wider than any vault in Europe — is 90 feet high and nearly 150 feet deep.

35 The great palace at Bishapur, also built by Shapur about the time of his victory over the Roman Emperor Valerian (260 A.D.), is a more complex ivan-type structure. The audience hall, 72 feet square, was vaulted with a dome 80 feet high. Each side is an arrangement of triple ivans. Built of stone and brick rubble set in mortar, the extensive stucco decoration of this palace provides the best extant examples of the interior decoration of a Sasanian palace. Many decorative motifs are borrowed from Greco-Roman prototypes — Shapur had taken thousands of Roman prisoners — but, as Ghirshman points out, here rather happily comdined with Persian taste and tradition

Sarvistan, reconstruction

In the fifth century palace built by Bahram V at Sarvistan a more complex development and expanded technique is evident. The central ivan of the eastern façade provides access to the central domed chamber and a square court whose single ivan is placed on the central axis in the blind western wall. Although reminiscent of Firuzabad, here there is more freedom and far less symmetry. *33*

Squinches were used to support the round domes, in addition to the use of columns as supports for the vaulting in the side rooms.

Unfortunately, most known Sasanian buildings are even more ruined than these, and although ground plans can be redrawn from archaeological evidence, their actual appearance remains conjectural. Palaces at Kish, Damghan, Haush Quri and Qasr-i-Shirin serve mainly as evidence that our knowledge of the full range of Sasanian architecture is far too incomplete. *34*

Despite the now ruined state of many Sasanian buildings, clues

Taq-i-Kisra, Ctesiphon

to the architectural ornament are provided by contemporary drawings on metal vessels. Decoration had expanded since Achaemenid times, becoming more ornate and more lavishly disposed. Designing the stucco ornamentation independently of the architecture and casting it in repeating molds encouraged a separation of decoration and structure. Facing the arches with busts in full round was a form of decoration later copied in European medieval architecture.

Takht-i-Suleiman, *see* 37, Southeast Gate

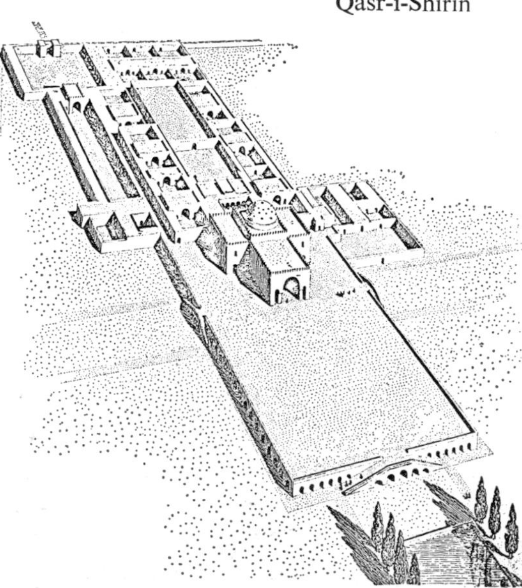

Qasr-i-Shirin

Bishapur, model of palace

The colors retained in several sites, Kuh-i-Khwaja or Bishapur, are of surprising range: red, yellow, turquoise, dull blue, light green, purple, violet, orange, fleshcolor, and white. Walls and barrel vaults were covered with mural paintings — sometimes executed in true fresco technique — depicting battles, hunting scenes, excursions. Floors and walls were also treated with mosaics, large in scale, rich in color.

Bishapur, mosaics

Sasanian fire temples and sanctuaries of a cult some thousands of years old—and preceding the coming of the Aryans, as Japanese excavations in Marv-i-Dasht show — were scattered through the Sasanian empire. The forms were similar — a dome on squinches placed over a square formed by four large piers connected with arches.

The Sasanian fire temples were so simple and forceful that they exerted a marked influence both East and West. In Buddhist territories, its ample interior space was adopted as a "hollow stupa", used for worship and filled with images of Buddha. There were Christian churches in many places in the Sasanian empire (only three excavated: Ctesiphon, Hera and Rusafa). The so-called "cross within a square" plan is essentially so close to a fire temple that one temple was used alternately by Christians and Sasanians. Christian acceptance of a Sasanian architectural type reached medieval Europe and exerted a marked effect on Romanesque architecture.

No single monument can be appraised in historic isolation; for adequate appreciation a monument must take its place in relation to others of its kind. Frequently, of course, this is scarcely possible. But we can fill the gap a bit with evidence left by documents, traditions and sundry artifacts.

These yield us some understanding of a remarkable Sasanian building: the Takht-i-Taqdis, on a sacred mountaintop in northwest Persia, a point of contact between heaven and earth, the reputed birthplace of Zoroaster and the most sacred shrine in the Sasanian world. Formerly known as Shiz or Ganzaca, it is today called Takht-i-Suleiman, the Throne of Solomon. As the Takht-i-Taqdis it was in existence only a few years, having been built by Chosroes II in 618 and destroyed by the Byzantine Emperor Heraclius in 628.

37

It is at least possible that this building provided the initial concept of the Castle of Holy Grail. It is especially significant for the history of Persian architecture because it expressed so specifically the ancient Persian theory of the function of the throne as intermediary between heaven and earth — as at Persepolis, effected by sympathetic magic — reproducing the firmament with a verisimilitude that was to compel sympathetic response from the heavens. The whole building, described by many Arabic, Persian and Byzantine sources, was set on rollers so that it could be turned in correspondence with the rotating sky. Even more significant was the reported apparatus for creating mock storms: machines for lightning, thunder and rain to induce the outer heavens to send life-giving storms to replenish the earth.

Takht-i-Suleiman, reconstruction, *see* 34

The building shown on the famous "Fortress Plate" in Leningrad rests on a masonry foundation identical to that of the wall of Takht-i-Suleiman. The little concentric half circles that unite the columns on the façade of the Fortress Plate are conspicuous over the main gate at Takht-i-Suleiman. This seems to support the recent theory that the building represented on the plate was really at Takht-i-Suleiman.

With limited architectural resources, Sasanian builders suddenly had to meet urgent demands from the new dynasty to proclaim itself as promptly as possible with impressive monuments. Despite these handicaps some imposing buildings were achieved and some splendid ruins exist today. The most important Sasanian contributions were in the development of the dome and its setting on squinches, in huge vaults built without centering and the division of massive weights into structural functions, the concentration of loads on separate fixed points and the suggestive use of transverse vaults. All were significant for Western developments and were fully deployed in subsequent Islamic architecture. As Oskar Reuther pointed out, "This is a first tentative step towards the constructional system of which Gothic architecture is the supreme realization."

IV. THE SIMPLE AND THE NOBLE

EARLY ISLAM: 650-1000 A.D.

With the speed and violence of a desert whirlwind, the Arabs burst out of their ancestral homes, shattered Persian military power at Nihavand in 637 A.D. and, within a few years, sent the surviving Sasanian rulers fleeing to China. Surprisingly, the continuity of Persian life was not really severed; essential elements of Sasanian culture continued to operate. The conquering forces of Islam imposed no architecture because they had none to impose. However, Sasanian architecture — inventive, audacious, impressive as it was — because of its somewhat elemental structural forms had relied too heavily upon inert masses for stability. It was the achievement of Islamic Persia to refine these powerful forms and to develop their potentials into an architecture of exceeding beauty. The result was to be lighter, more sensitive, more varied and more expressive than its antecedents.

The organization of the Islamic empire, dominating a culturally diverse area, opened new avenues of communication, augmenting commerce, and creating an expanding economy which in time supplied the wealth needed for a new and urgent era of building — both secular and religious. Mosques, colleges, tombs, bridges, forts, hospitals, caravanserais and libraries were needed everywhere.

Islam proclaimed both the brotherhood of all and the fatherhood of God, giving a new dignity and value to the common man. In Persia, conversion to Islam was not so much by the sword as by persuasion. Islam became the central and conspicuous fact in the Persian mind. Replacing the grandiose palaces that had so ostentatiously proclaimed the pride and power of kings, the mosque, with its more communal and democratic character, became as immediate and important as the cathedral in medieval Europe.

From the mosque five times a day came the call to communal prayer, and on Friday the call for attendance. But the mosque is open to all people at any time. It belongs to all Moslems on an equal basis, and the homeless wanderer has the same claim on its

Tari-Khana, Damghan, 8th century

spiritual and physical hospitality as the proudest resident prince. Even today, incoming caravans repair immediately to the mosque where access is never questioned and any vagabond may sleep. Moreover, the mosque became the basic educational institution, from elementary grades through sophisticated philosophy, and popular lectures. A college, *madrassa*, was often attached, and each mosque had its own library.

The mosque was often a court of justice. Scribes did a flourishing business there. Parts of the mosque complex were even used as prisons or morgues. Spiritually coextensive with the whole life of the people, the mosque often becomes physically integrated with the city — indeed can become its very focus. With its various appendages it was a veritable *civitas Dei* set in the midst of the *civitas mundi*. In cases where this integration of the two worlds was complete, the mosque merged with surrounding buildings. Hence it had neither external walls nor façade, save for the portal, and its area was frequently difficult to define.

Architecturally the mosque may be wholly an interior court design, conceived to exclude the outer world and emphasize its inner concentration. Repetitive elements — arcades or columns — give it coherence and at the same time define its purpose: fulfillment of the deepest kind of unity. In the mosque is focused the life and meaning of the community.

Almost immediately after the advent of Islam in Iran, there was a great surge of building. New religious and secular buildings were continuously required, and they had to be created out of local materials, techniques and styles. To be sure, no Persian building from the first two Islamic centuries has survived, but contemporary descriptions tell us much. Thus, we know these earliest mosques, often ambitious undertakings involving great expense, continued ancient Persian architectural traditions of sumptuous ornament.

There were three basic mosque types:

31 *the pavilion* — a dome over a square chamber (the Sasanian fire temple adapted to Islamic ritual);

34 *the open ivan* — simple barrel vault, tradition of Taq-i-Kisra;

39 *the open court* (so-called Arab plan) surrounded by arcades.

Eventually, all three types were merged. Within three centuries, many important mosques, to say nothing of caravanserais, bazaars, and other types of structures, were built. Little survives, but contemporary accounts speak of these mosques with enthusiasm for their beauty, lavish decoration and impressive size. For such a building program Persia was able to supply competent, experienced architects who, under the Sasanians, had been grounded in the already long traditions of Persian architecture. Even as late as the fourteenth century Sasanian structures were still conspicuous

Carved stucco, Nishapur, 10th century

throughout the land, providing ideas and serving as models for new structures. The vast arch of Ctesiphon repeatedly stirred rulers to emulation, challenging the capacities of architects for more than a thousand years; and the solid, solemn fire temples were readily adapted to serve as tombs, *Imamzadas*, of the venerated saints.

Except for a few crumbling walls and archaeologically revealed ground plans, the oldest existing Islamic structure in Persia is the 39 little Tari-Khana in Damghan, built about 760. The layout is the typical inner-court plan: a large, almost square, court surrounded by arcades of tunnel vaults set on huge round piers $11\frac{1}{2}$ feet high and almost 6 feet in diameter. The whole design is simple, it gives and "impression of grandeur and sovereign beauty; one of the most magnificent buildings in Islam". It is a purely Sasanian building.

The only innovation lies in the slightly pointed arches, the first recorded in Persia. Even the radial lay, the dimensions of the burnt bricks and the columns themselves are identical to the nearby Sasanian palace.

In their present somber state, the earliest Islamic monuments would seem to their builders impoverished and monotonous, for the architecture of the period was already committed to rich decorative effects, exuberant but sophisticated polychromed stucco. The earliest remaining fragments — from Nishapur, probably late eighth century; from the Masjid-i-Jami in Shiraz, late ninth century; and from the Masjid-i-Jami in Nayin, mid-tenth century — are of great *41* beauty and elegance. The mosque at Nishapur had marble columns, gold tiles, polychrome carved stucco walls and profusely ornamented roofs. At Damghan "magnificent ornaments with precious marble" were used. From Parthian times on, carved and polychromed stucco was a major factor in architectural embellishment.

Masjid-i-Jami, Nayin

THE SAMANIDS: 892-999 A.D.

The final acceptance of Islam brought a much needed peace, the economic basis for creative energies. By the second half of the ninth century a genuine Persian renaissance was developing in Khurasan (which then included Transoxiana and Afghanistan). Under the brilliant Samanid dynasty claiming Sasanian ancestry, from Bokhara and Samarkand throughout the tenth century, a new yet characteristically Persian culture emerged, one of the most exceptional and creative in Persian history.

Tomb of Ismail Samanid, Bokhara, 907

How the proportions work

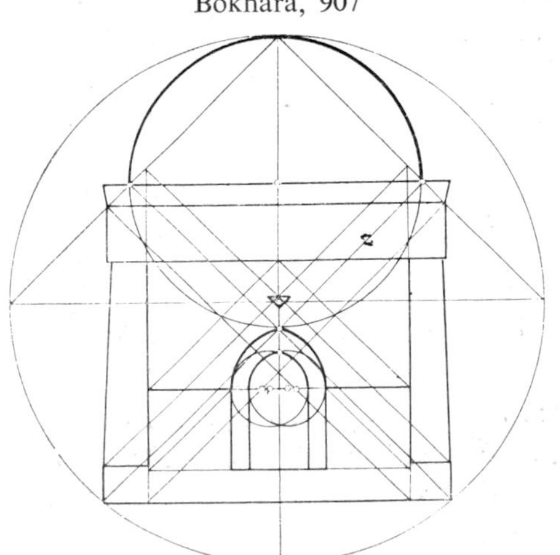

Only one monument survives, but that one of the finest in Persia: the mausoleum of Ismail Samanid in Bokhara (USSR). Both in structural development and in its brilliant decorative deployment of material it exerted a strong influence on subsequent Islamic architecture. Simple and impressive in scale (although actually a small building), its harmonious and thoroughly studied proportions, its vigorous and inventive ornamentation, combine to rank it among the masterpieces of Persian architecture. *42* *42*

Judging by the number of buildings reported to have collapsed during the first centuries of Islam, the techniques necessary for stability of domes had not been fully developed prior to Ismail's tomb. Setting a dome over a square chamber is here carried beyond the simple solution of Parthian and Sasanian times. The rib in the squinch carries the thrust of the dome downward — somewhat in the fashion of a Gothic flying buttress.

Quite as commanding as the powerful form and robust construction is the decorative energy of the surfaces. Brick was used with a vivacity and intensity that had no precedent. The deeply shadowed texture of the walls, recalling wicker-work, veils the harsh reflected glare of sunlight. Much of the ornament seems derived

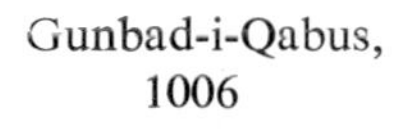

Gunbad-i-Qabus, 1006

Bayazid, Bistam, 1313

Pir-i-Alamdar, 1021

from carved wood techniques — a confirmation of statements by Istakhri that a good deal of wood was used in these early mosques.

In Turan, this impressive monument was followed by a whole series in a somewhat similar style, and early Mongol architecture continues many of the same features.

Under the shadow of the eastern Elburz mountains, facing the vastness of the Asian steppes, stands in stark majesty a supreme 43 architectural masterpiece: the Gunbad-i-Qabus, the tomb tower of Qabus-ibn Washmgir. It rises a full 167 feet, with another 35 feet or so underground, of time-defying hard-fired brick, now bronze and golden tan in color. Ten powerful right-angled flanges project from the circular body, vertically uniting base and roof. Kufic inscription panels between each flange (at the top and near the bottom) tell us that it was built by Qabus in 1006-7. Qabus was an extraordinary man, ruling Gurgan intermittently from 976 to about 1012. A scholar and patron of scholars, a poet and patron of poets, a calligrapher, astrologer, linguist, chess player and doughty warrior, he was also unreasonably suspicious and, in the end, was assassinated by his exasperated nobles. The monumental shaft is stripped clean, a warrior in mortal combat with Fate, as it were, a monarch-poet wrestling with eternity. Is there any funerary monument so expressive, so commanding?

The Gunbad-i-Qabus is the earliest and most expressive of a series of some fifty monumental towers still standing. These cover a period of seven hundred years, vary enormously in size, form and ornamentation. They have been found in nearly every part of Persia. The great majority are round, beginning with the tomb 43 tower of Pir-i-Alamdar (1021) at Damghan and at Lajim, Mazanderan (1022). Towers with prismatic flanges like the Gunbad-i-Qabus continue through the twelfth century at Rayy (1139) and 43 into the fourteenth with that at Bistam (1313). An important group in which the body of the tower is composed of an engaged cluster of almost round shafts is at Jar Kugan, at Radkan East (1280-1300), and at Kishmar (fourteenth century). Coupled columns begin with the Rabat-i-Malek, or the tower at Jar Kugan, reappear in the Kutb Minar of Delhi. A few towers are octagonal, beginning with the Gunbad-i-Ali at Abarquh, (1036), the superb 46-7 pair at Kharagan (1067-1093) continuing through the fourteenth century in tombs at Qumm and the Imamzada Jafar at Isfahan (1341) and even later. Some are square, such as the Gunbad-i-Surkh at Maragha (eleventh century) and the tomb of Shahzada Muhammed at Sari in Mazandaran (fifteenth century).

These towers faithfully reflect period, local styles and the genius of individual architects. The rugged Gunbad-i-Ali (1056) at Abarquh, crowning an abrupt little eminence, is built of heavy rubble and its walls show a decided entasis. The earlier towers of Maragha (a special study in themselves) are masterpieces of brick construction and compact energetic form — particularly the square Gunbad-i-Surkh (1147) which, with its ingeniously designed brick patterns and its ponderous corner column, recalls the tomb of 42 Ismail Samanid. Its secondary ornamentation consists of inset carved terra-cotta panels placed above the arched panels. Later examples are more lavishly decorated, for instance the Gunbad-i-Kabud (1196) which has sunken pointed arched panels on each face, the whole overlaid by a geometrical framework in blue faience and enriched by a dense stalactite cornice and a blue on white inscription band. This sumptuous combination is saved from weakness by the massive form and stout engaged columns framing the panels.

Another remarkable minaret built *circa* 1179 by the Ghorid Sultan Ghi ad-Din at Jam in Afghanistan, rises spectacularly out 47 of the heart of a deep rocky gorge. It is two hundred feet high, in three stages of studied proportions and firm stance. Densely covered with deeply cut stucco of an especially rich counterpoint of floral and geometric ornament wrapped around interweaving bands of a Kufic inscription which contains a whole chapter of the Koran, the *Maryam sutra* — 973 words! The minaret is in perfect condition, save for two flaring platforms that have broken away. It is a work of mind and spirit, an exultation and commemoration of military and political triumph, confronting and dominating the bleak mass of unfeeling rock around it. It is a work of psychic intensity.

Scattered all through the province of Mazanderan and up into the Elburz Mountains are some striking and often handsome tomb towers, frequently combined with mosques. Of rustic local style they are often quite touching in their simplicity. The best, however, are from the fifteenth century and most are distinguished as a simple mass with a top frieze of slightly corbeled blind arcades. They sometimes have an astonishing similarity to eleventh century Romanesque towers. Of native brick, some are even plastered.

Mostly bordering the southern gulf and on islands such as Karg, is a very striking tower form resembling a sugar loaf. These con- 47 sist of some ten or fifteen receding courses of plain convex panels stacked one on top of another in diminishing sizes, rising to quite a sharp point — an architectural fantasy that has a good deal of charm. Their history is still to be written; their dates uncertain.

Palace at Tashan

Damghan, 1026

Tomb tower, Kharagan, 1093

"Sugar-loaf" towers, Karg

Minaret of Jam, 1179

Tomb tower, Kharagan, 1067

THE GHAZNAVIDS: 962-1040 A.D.

The renaissance of Persian culture initiated under the Samanids was transmitted to their successors, the warlike Ghaznavids, in the form of architectural ambitions and traditions, sophisticated taste, and enthusiasm for literature, science and art. Mahmud of Ghazna (997-1030), lavished immense sums and great energy, utilizing workmen from all quarters of his realm on sumptuous architecture. Only two victory towers and the impressive ruins of Lashkari Bazar remain. The poet, Nizami-Aruzi, tells us a lot in three lines:

> How many a palace did great Mahmud raise
> At whose tall towers the Moon did stand agaze
> Whereof one brick remaineth not in place.

CENTRAL PERSIA — THE BUYIDS: 935-1055 A.D.

Central Persia under the Buyids was simultaneously developing a different cultural pattern, apparently animated by the finest Iranian traditions. Of buildings, almost nothing remains, though by at least the tenth century extensive and monumental buildings were in northern Khuzistan. This extremely difficult terrain has defied any full-scale exploration as yet, although Aurel Stein incidentally *46* noted some ruined structures near Tashan. These, briefly studied by a helicopter expedition of the Asia Institute, reveal a great palatial complex—domed, vaulted, rubble-built—of about 30 acres. Contemporary structures were found in and near Bonevar, including a palatial fort crowning an abrupt peak, surrounded by some cultivatable land, the whole isolated, self-sustaining, practically invulnerable; accessible only though narrow gorges equipped with ladders.

An architectural style was forming in Shiraz and Isfahan. The Jurjir mosque, of which only a portal remains—with no color other than the golden ivory tone that comes from its exclusive use of plaster—was accordingly to reports very beautiful, but too fragile to endure. Adud ad-Dawla's palace library in Shiraz, a vaulted two-story building had 360 rooms, each of different shape, each decorated in different style and color.

51 Aside from sections of the Masjid-i-Jami in Isfahan, the oldest standing monument representing this new dispensation is the Shrine of the Davazdah Imam in Yazd, dated 1036. Here, the ancient problem of setting the dome on a square is all but perfectly solved, to be carried to perfection in Seljuk Isfahan.

V. STRUCTURE AS BEAUTY

THE SELJUKS: 1000-1157 A.D.

Seljuk architecture, noble and powerful, structurally inventive and sophisticated, was neither sudden nor accidental. Rather it was the culminating expression of a Persian renaissance that had begun in the early tenth century with the Samanids. This renaissance reached its apex under the Seljuks.

CULTURAL BACKGROUND

"Seek ye knowledge even unto China," commanded the Prophet Muhammed and, next to prayer, learning was regarded as most sacred, preferable even to unreasoned piety. The productive stimulation of different, and often competing, societies was steadily enlarging and energizing Islamic cultural life and thought. Most significant was the appropriation and preservation of classical Greek culture. Through well-organized translations financed by Caliph Mamun (813-833), Greek philosophy and science became known in Persia. Galen, Plato and Aristotle were assiduously studied by all leaders of Persian thought.

During the tenth century, however, Persia again produced its own constellation of poets, philosophers, mathematicians, astronomers, physical scientists, historians, geographers and lexicographers — most of them brilliant, many of unequaled eminence, all with a high degree of originality, boldness and cultural breadth. In comparison, the same years in Europe were dark indeed.

By far the most important element in the initiation of the native Persian revival was Firdawsi's poem the *Shah Nama*, completed in 1010. One of the world's greatest epics, it entered immediately and permanently into the heart of the nation. In all of his sixty thousand couplets he used no more than nine hundred and eighty-four Arabic expressions; the rest were purely Persian. He restored to the Persians the use of a renovated magnificent language, created new confidence and patriotism.

The rulers, a number of them true scholars and even poets, rivaled each other in patronizing poets, artists and scholars. The honor of being a patron was regarded as an obligation of royalty and a valid claim to status and public esteem. The libraries of the time tell the story of a widely shared culture, in which learning was revered. Sahib ibn Abbad, vizier of the Buyids and successful ruler of most of Persia before his death in 996, had a vast library of certainly more than two hundred thousand volumes. Each mosque had a collection of books, and magistrates were encouraged to collect and preserve them. The Cadi of Nishapur designated a house with a library especially for the use of visiting scholars, and even supplied them with living expenses. One famous library was compiled by Adud ad-dawla installed in a special building in Shiraz.

Both the Buyid and Seljuk periods produced some of the most remarkable textiles ever achieved and the pottery, mostly from Nishapur and Samarkand, is among the finest ever made.

The second half of the ninth century saw the appearance of a number of encyclopaedias and general histories. The learned professions produced a number of great thinkers, competent in several areas: Al Razi (*circa* 850-923), physician, chemist and physicist whose influence spread to make itself felt in Renaissance Europe. His ablest colleagues were mostly Persian. Al Tabari's (838-923), ten-volume history of music contained much valuable historical and even archaeological material. He created a systematic star catalogue, astronomical tables and ingenious astronomical instruments. Mathematics and astronomy were vigorously summarized in a Persian encyclopaedia of 976, *The Keys of the Sciences.* A group called the "Brethren of Sincerity", published valuable commentaries.

Ibn Sina (Avicenna, 980-1037) was a born mathematician, poet and astronomer who made important contributions to physics and was one of the world's first great figures in medicine and the related field of pharmacology, and his medical treatises were basic texts at Oxford and Montpellier as late as the seventeenth century.

Omar Khayyam was also an original philosopher and a great mathematician. He recognized thirteen different forms of cubic equations (with suggested solutions) and, in 1074, formulated a new calendar of "remarkable accuracy, probably better than our own". Al Ghazali (1038-1111), a man of intellectual power, deep feeling and utter dedication, was outstanding as poet, philosopher and theologian but, in the spirit of the times, he also had working knowledge of a number of the sciences and wrote original astrological treatises and a general summary of astronomy.

Into this highly developed civilization came the conquering Seljuks, an Irano-Turkish stock, their leaders already familiar with the Persian culture established in Central Asia.

Masjid-i-Jami, Isfahan, sanctuary dome (minaret, 15th cent.)

SELJUK ARCHITECTURE

Seljuk architecture in Persia, scarcely recognized as a distinct style before 1930, now comprises a repertoire of about fifty monuments and is increasingly regarded as one of the world's great architectural styles. A number of important monuments have been recorded within the last decade; still more may come to light. Each discovery reveals new merits in structural inventiveness: double domes, ribs, wider vaults, taller minarets: and in decoration: stucco mihrabs, opulent and expressive overall arabesque networks, and in brick ornamentation patterns and bondings of infinite variety, vigor and originality.

The power and nobility of Seljuk architecture is doubtless best exemplified by the Masjid-i-Jami of Isfahan, one of the greatest buildings in the world. As a magnificent structure in a city chosen to be Persia's capital during widely separated epochs and under a variety of rulers, the Isfahan Jami is not purely Seljuk, but those portions which date from Seljuk times are yet its chief glories.

More than 900 years of Persian architecture are revealed in this great mosque's twenty distinct structures, varying in date from the eleventh to eighteenth centuries. During its long history it has been much fought over, repeatedly damaged, reconstructed, and all but ruined. Nevertheless, it endured all and in its thirty or so historical inscriptions — still not perfectly interpreted — it adds documentation to our appreciation of its majestic forms.

A four-ivan court (196 × 230 feet) is enclosed by arcades and *57* two-story open galleries faced with mosaic faience on buff brick. A deep ivan, embellished with especially strong faience revetments opens into a spacious domed sanctuary built, as the inscription states, by order of Nizam al-mulk at the beginning of Malik Shah's reign (1072, almost certainly before 1075). Some of the earlier buildings are still visible, however, and it is probable that the lower section of this sanctuary itself dates from the late tenth century. This chamber — spacious and noble, of compelling grandeur — supports a huge dome, 50 feet in diameter, which rests on deep tri-lobed squinches (their form developed from the Buyid Davazdah Imam of Yazd). The squinches, in turn, are supported by huge cylindrical piers that are crowned by Abbasid-looking stucco scrolls, certainly of earlier date than the dome. The sanctuary is surround- *53* ed by arcades and corridors covered by an amazing variety of *55* domical brick vaults, some with stont ribs and an independent supporting framework in the Gothic manner (thus indicating the possibility of a contributory relation). Frequently these vaults rest on columns that vary in date from pre-Seljuk to the Safavid period. All of the ivans were rebuilt or redecorated on a Seljuk base, showing that the basic plan of the Jami existed during the Seljuk period.

Aesthetically, the most important unit in the Jami is the small *54* but superlative north dome known as the Gunbad-i-Kharka, dated 1088, and located at the opposite end of the central axis from the sanctuary. This is perhaps the most perfect dome known. Its solemn, memory-gripping power is not a matter of dimensions (65 feet high and 35 feet in diameter), but of design. Every feature has been meticulously studied and, with the perfection of a sonnet, fused into a completely unified whole. Mechanically it matches the mathematical requirements of the ideal dome, achieving an accuracy at critical points that approaches exact duplication. In each corner,

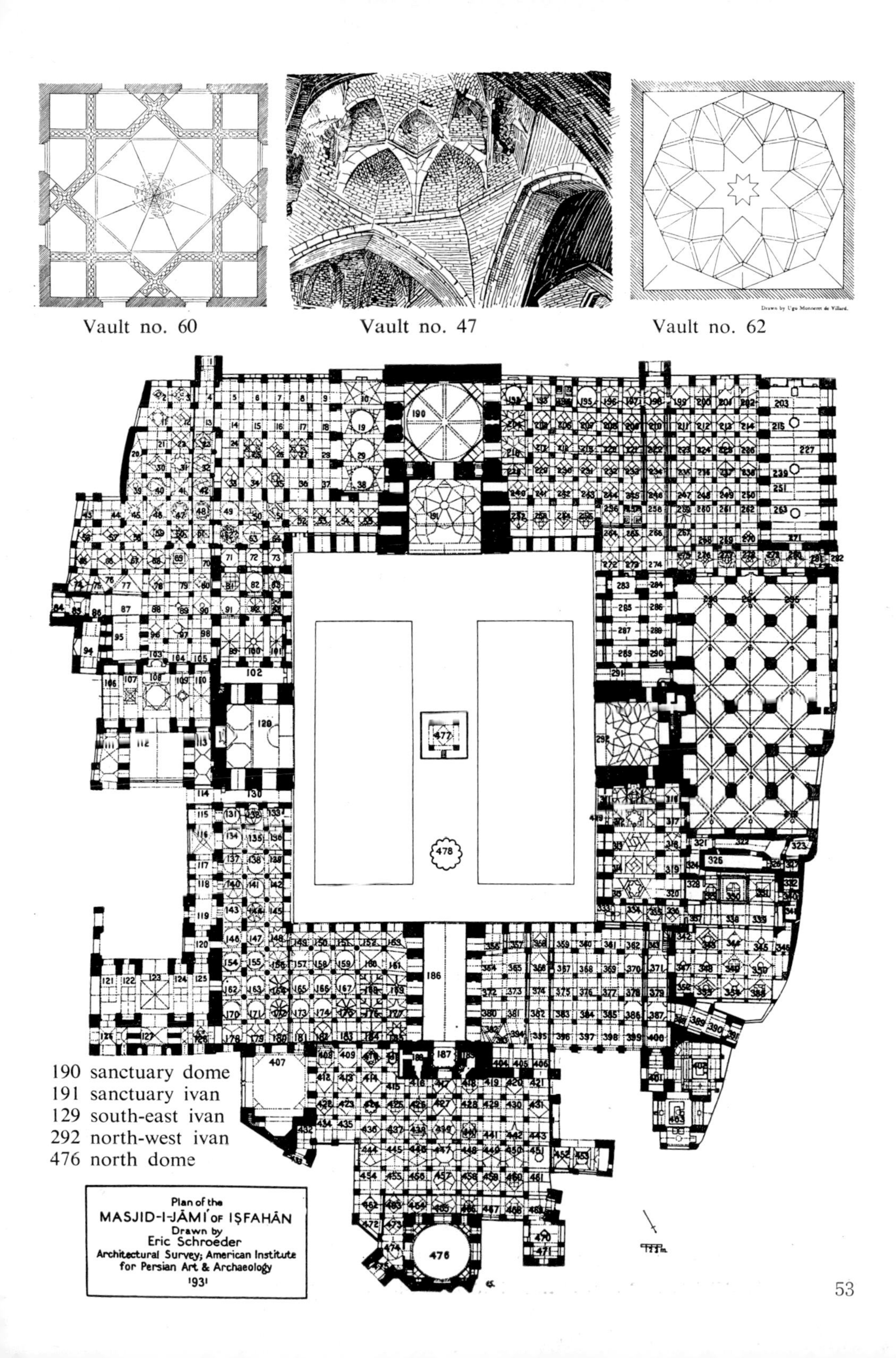

Vault no. 60

Vault no. 47

Vault no. 62

Masjid-i-Jami, Isfahan

north dome chamber
(Gunbad-i-Kharka), 1088

above, right cross-section

above left, dome and squinch
west corner and squinch

opposite:
south corner vault
sanctuary (interior), 107
north-east vaults, 12th cen

four narrow arched recesses framed by slender angle colonettes form the downward extension of the squinch. From floor level, *54* these colonettes lead the eye swiftly up to the typical tri-lobed squinch. The squinch itself is enclosed by a larger arch that, together with identical arches along the side walls, supports an octagonal ring of sixteen shallow panels merged with the base of the dome.

All arch forms, including the dome, are of the same contour and constitute the key element or motif that, beginning in the corners, with successive comprehensiveness enclose one element within the other until their multiplicity is resolved and merged in the dome — the inevitable conclusion of the complex upward movement. The dome is thus the culminating point in a vertically rising stream of force. Such natural and logical succession of identical forms, so precisely defined, endows this space with a compactness and perfect unity that makes it as moving as anything in Persian architecture. The subdued bronze color of the brick, relieved only by inconspicuous dark gray and white carved terracotta insets, adds to the solemn impression. The sense of utter finality, however, comes from the perfection of form tself. This single-shell dome, having survived without a crack for almost 900 years in a country of earthquakes, is proof of its "subtle mathematics and impeccable mechanism". Like the Gunbad-i-Qabus, it was "built for eternity".

There are some significant features of the building which are easily overlooked. The ceiling of the dome is ornamented by a *54* huge cinquefoil in low relief which is assimilated to a five-pointed star. A section of this motif (an isosceles triangle) penetrates at five spaced intervals from the periphery. Simple though it be, it is a pattern of noble beauty consonant with the building of which it is the crown — the final triumph of the whole process by which the square ground plan finally merges with the dome.

opp: inscription in
braided Kufic
north-east ivan
c. 1310

North-west ivan
— rear and
— front views

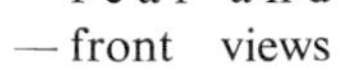

Masjid-i-Jami, Qazvin

A beautiful little madrassa, the Hedariya (early twelfth century) is also in Qazvin, today incorporated into a larger nineteenth century mosque. Perhaps the finest Kufic inscription in relief in all Persia is in its stucco frieze. Its carved stucco mihrab is massively rich. The large Masjid-i-Jami at Qazvin (1113-15) is impressive by virtue of its serene sanctuary space, capped by a large dome (52 feet in diameter). The groined squinch, framed by a powerful arch, is almost primitive in its emptiness. Its inscriptions rival Hedariya's.

Several important Seljuk mosques, in the style of the Isfahan Jami survive in relatively good condition: the Friday mosques at Ardistan (*circa* 1180), Zaware (1153) and Gulpayagan (1120-35), and the Shrine of Bayazid at Bistam, a brick minaret (*circa* 1120).

Rabat-i-Malek, *c.* 1078

These great Seljuk monuments of Central Persia were rivaled by several structures built to the northeast, in Khurasan and the region of the Oxus. Of these, the gigantic Rabat-i-Malek built before 1078 between Bukhara and Samarkand, is one of the most imposing ruins of the Islamic period. Only part of one wall of this caravanserai remains. This fragment alone suffices to show that here (possibly as early as the first half of the eleventh century) was built a massive and forbidding structure of plain brick, simple as becomes a frontier fortress.

59

Sultan Sanjar was buried at Merv in a mausoleum worthy of a noble and tragic figure. Constructed after his death in 1157 by a devoted follower, this tomb is a ponderous and solemn cubical chamber, about 90 feet square and was surmounted by a blue-tiled dome (now partly collapsed), also about 90 feet high. The interlocking framework of the ribs seen on the interior seems to carry the weight of the dome but, in reality, it may be more decorative than structural. Brick latticework at the corners admitted light to the corridor around the base of the dome, a further development of the tomb of Ismail Samanid and one that anticipates the mausoleum of Uljaitu at Sultaniya. The plain walls are enriched with a typically Seljuk plaster coating marked out in simulated brick bonding with decorative insets of terracotta. This mausoleum is the last, and one of the finest, examples of Seljuk architecture.

Decoration evocative of vegetation, mosaic faience, Gaupier, Isfahan, 16th cent

61 Rivaling stucco was the impressive development of enameled tile, Persia's greatest contribution to ornament. The luster faience

Tile, overglaze painted and gilded with relief
showing Bahram Gur and Azada, Kashan, 13th cent.

mihrabs appearing late in the thirteenth century were exquisitely startling. The use of tiny fragments of cut tile in Maragha carly in the twelfth century suggested the possibilities of combining finely divided units of such tiles in intricate patterns instead of the earlier single, solid colored tiles. Luster faience differs in having a second coating of metallic salts which in the second firing brings about an irridescent quality. Fragile, it is usually limited to use in interiors. *60*

VI. DESTRUCTION AND GRANDEUR

THE MONGOL IL KHANIDS: 1218-1334 A.D.

The Mongol invasions, begun by the ferocious Genghis Khan in 1218, with blind destructiveness ruined the lands they conquered, striking a near-fatal blow from which Persia never fully recovered. But by mid-century — tamed and instructed by Persian culture, by Islam and even Buddhism — Hulagu Khan (1217-65), grandson of Genghis, chief of the west, began to think of building.

Basic plans and structural types remained traditional and, specifically, Seljuk, but the proud and ambitious Mongol princes were determined to surpass everything that had preceded them. They had conquered the world, destroying much of it, and would now try to parallel that achievement by expressing their mastery in visible and permanent form. An increased scale became apparent: domes were of immense size and towers very high. Façades were energized by groups of tall, narrow pointed arched panels, a revival of parallel salients and recesses that alleviated the mass of the early ziggurats and temples, now artfully composed in groups of three. There was also a marked intensification of the old Persian verticality and exceedingly tall and narrow portals were much favored.

Hulagu ordered the reconstruction of some ruined cities, such as Kuchan, built himself a fine palace, a Buddhist temple at Khoy and about 1260 established at huge cost the famous observatory at Maragha. Under Arghun Khan (1281-92) architecture began to revive on a substantial scale. These rulers were by turns Buddhists, Christians, Sunnis and Shi'ites, shifts which were reflected in the erection of a number of Christian churches and monasteries as well as in the reconstruction of the lofty ivan at Takht-i-Suleiman under Abaqa Khan about 1275. Ghazan Khan (1295-1304), a fervent convert to Islam refined under Persian tutelage, ranks as one of Persia's greatest rulers and innovators, initiator of a new and important period in Persian architecture. As he himself said, "I inherited a ruined country," but once his regime was consolidated, he and his associates planned with such limitless enthusiasm and built with such furious energy, irrespective of cost, that within a decade they had created a series of superb monuments.

Typical was his order that a mosque and bath should be built in each town, the profits from the bath to support the mosque. His greatest achievement was the suburb of Sham, two miles south of Tabriz — in variety, organization and magnitude hardly rivaled by anything since Persepolis. Today only rubble, it was once a complex of monasteries, madrassas, a hospital, library, philosophical academy, administrative palace, observatory and palatial summer residences, as well as arcades and gardens of exceptional charm. Fourteen thousand workmen worked four years to complete the structure, which was still standing, only slightly damaged, four hundred years later despite severe and frequent earthquakes. Rashid ad-Din, Ghazan's vizier, created a university city in Tabriz that surpassed even the ancient complexes. It included twenty-four caravanserais, fifteen hundred shops, thirty thousand houses, special quarters for scholars who assembled there from all countries, hospitals, dispensaries and gardens — "for solidity and strength" surpassing all comparable structures.

By the command of Uljaitu, Ghazan's younger brother and successor (1304-16), there arose on the beautiful open meadows of Sultaniya a wonder city planned to be the imperial capital. Begun in 1305 and dedicated in 1313, it was built magnificently as well as rapidly. The result was a complex almost the size of Tabriz, dominated by Uljaitu's mausoleum, one of Persia's supreme architectural achievements. *64,67* The building was the climax of a congeries of subordinate buildings no longer extant. At one time it was planned to receive the bodies of Ali and Hussein, early saints revered by Persian Shi'ites, but this was given up, partly because of Uljaitu's conversion to the Sunni branch of Islam.

The mausoleum is octagonal in form, rising to a beautifully poised, high profile dome, 177 feet high and 80 feet in diameter, solidly covered with light blue faience tile. It rests on a wide and rich stalactite cornice and a gleaming blue-patterned minaret rose from each of the eight angles, framing the dome like a diadem. The second-story galleries open outward, anticipating the Khwaja *65* Rabi, Gadam Gah, and the Taj Mahal. Its imposing scale provides for an interior of great power. Here space is ample and majestic — not mere emptiness but space more intensely realized than an open landscape. The walls, though 23 feet thick, are made less conspicuous by the stately rhythm of eight huge and soaring arches. Mediated by shallow stalactites, the angles between these arches seem to melt quietly into the circular base of the enormous dome. All components are fused into a unity of serene grandeur. Despite

Mausoleum of Uljaitu, Sultaniya

— galleries, simulated brick and stucco

its size, the dome is as buoyant, as light and secure as the vault of heaven which it brings to mind.

The walls were originally faced with light golden-toned brick, punctuated with small, dark blue faience tiles strung out to form large inscriptions of rectangular Kufic, but in 1313 the interior was redecorated with plaster. Designs were varied; huge lacy medallions or painted mosaic and floral patterns, sacred inscriptions proclaimed the divine message, their undulating scripts kept alive a gentle flowing movement. The vaults of the outer twenty-four galleries (three on a side) were decorated with painted panels of *65* intricate geometric ornament, exceedingly lovely in design and vibrant in color.

Throughout, structure and ornament were united: majestic scale, harmonious proportions, rich and glowing colors all combined in a quiet equilibrium, endowing the building with a unique presence. Structurally the building is a masterpiece. "Loads and thrusts are properly concentrated on a relatively small number of points," and the huge dome is the work of a consummate technician having been "built without buttresses, pinnacles or shoulders of any kind". The thickness of the dome shell diminishes from base toward apex, a necessity in terms of both lightness and stability. This diminution in thickness was obtained by a series of steps which would naturally give a rough and irregular profile to the dome. The architect overcame this, however, by providing a smooth auxiliary outer shell which could carry the glazed tile on an even and easy contour. The double dome, although unusual, was by no means a new idea, for there already existed the tomb towers of Kharagan, discovered in 1965, and some forty domical vaults in the Masjid-i-Jami of Isfahan, all with double domes.

At Sultaniya, the dome stands "simply by virtue of a perfectly conceived and constructed profile". Here grandeur and tranquility both dwarf and magnify; here man is both diminished and ennobled. There are larger enclosed spaces — the 17th century Gol Gunbad in Bishapour (India), the Pantheon in Rome — but perhaps none that combines in such transparent unity, power, repose and sovereign beauty. It is the visible realization of the poet's dream: "a palace as massive as the mountain, resplendent as the stars, wide as the land, lifting itself into the sky."

Among the many other fine monuments of the period, the mausoleum at Pir-i-Bakran near Isfahan (dated 1303, but rebuilt in 1312) is an impressive example of the single-ivan structure, still *34* reminiscent of the Taq-i-Kisra.

Mausoleum of Uljaitu, Sultaniya, reconstruction

Masjid-i-Jami, Yazd

68 In Yazd, the Masjid-i-Jami, like so many important mosques, was the focus of a complex of buildings of various periods and styles in various states of conservation. The site of a Sasanian fire temple, its major features, however, were begun in 1324 and continuously developed for forty years. A portal ivan opens into a court at right angles to the main axis. A high ivan vault, leading into the domed sanctuary, focused on one of the finest mosaic faience mihrabs (1365). On either side were oratories, both distinguished by transverse vaults at right angles to the longitudinal axis — a

Masjid-i-Jami, Kirman

brilliant innovation of Sasanian times that covers with adequate strength a wide span. The high walls thus relieved of structural function, it was possible (as in the south oratory) to cut windows into either end of the vault. The ivan and sanctuary are especially marked by the urge to verticality and the portal minarets are the highest in Iran. The Masjid-i-Jami of Kirman (dated 1349, rebuilt in 1559) also is a large four-ivan structure whose tall portal arch is rather similar to that at Yazd. Its richly patterned mosaic faience is of outstanding decorative energy. *69*

Almost concurrently, Ali Shah, a wealthy and ambitious patron of architecture said to have been the architect of Sham and the mausoleum of Uljaitu, began work on the Masjid-i-Jami in 70 Tabriz (begun 1312 and finished by 1322). We again find the colossal scale initiated by Ghazan Khan, for it is probably the most massive brick structure standing. The sanctuary ivan was a vault 100 feet wide and 158 feet deep; the distance between portal and mihrab was over 215 feet. The springing of the vault which must have been over 150 feet high, began about 80 feet from the ground, and it seems a pair of minarets rose to a height of more than 200 feet. The ivan portal faced a marble-paved court (937 × 750 feet), which was surrounded by a stone-vaulted arcade supported on coupled octagonal alabaster columns, richly decorated with gold. The largest doors (about 9 feet square) were closed by single slabs of polished alabaster. Arcades and ivans were faced with faience tile or mosaic faience and a huge inscription in gold and white against a floral ground wound around the entire building. The interior was equally sumptuous. All combined to create an ensemble of utmost splendor, sustained by the mass of the structure. The immense vault collapsed within a few years, although the building continued in use for several centuries.

Masjid-i-Jami, Tabriz, 1312-1322

Masjid-i-Jami, Veramin, 1322

In the early fourteenth century, the city of Varamin — like Natanz — became a center of building, having gained in importance with the decline of Rayy, so thoroughly devastated by earlier Mongols. The tomb tower of Ala ad-Din (1287) followed the typical northern scheme, with thirty-two right-angled flanges and a conical tiled roof, ornamented with an inscription frieze and a strapwork cornice band of the characteristic blue faience and terra cotta. The now ruined Masjid-as-Sharif (1307) leaves few traces of its former magnificence but the Masjid-i-Jami is still one of the most attractive mosques in the country, finished in 1326 under the last of the Il Khanid Mongols. Although unostentatious, it discloses a richly varied scheme of ornamentation, consisting of intricate patterns of blue faience strips relieved by buff terra cotta. Delicate diapers of shadow lines in the raised or cut-out brick trace out religious messages in huge rectangular Kufic, confirmed by deeply carved Naskhi inscription friezes. The piers are faced with painted plaster, narrow bands in carved stucco, all meticulously executed.

71

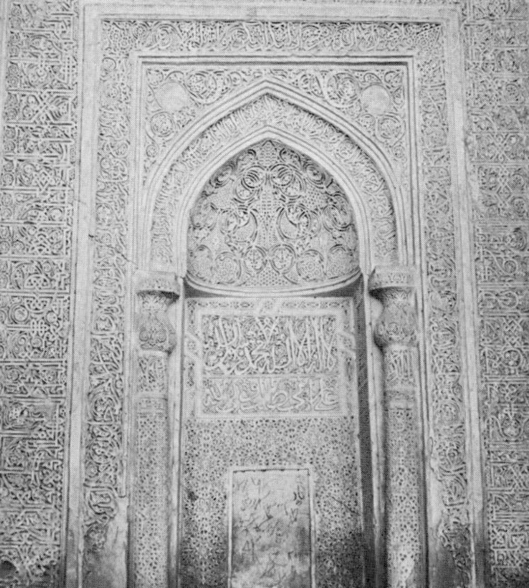

←Opposite: Shrine of Bayazid, Bistam; lower, door and mihrab

The revered shrine of Bayazid at Bistam (an assemblage ranging in date from the tenth century and including a minaret dated 1120 and an austere tomb tower of about 1300, similar in style to the Gunbad-i-Qabus but less austere), was further elaborated by Ghazan Khan and the young Uljaitu in the early fourteenth century with an outstanding stucco mihrab of 1267 and fine stucco panels. 72 43 43

A similar but more homogeneous complex of considerable beauty was built at Natanz, one of the loveliest mountain towns in Persia. Abrupt hills, ample trees, rushing streams and the remains of former palaces made it an ideal retreat for people from Kashan and Yazd, both fiercely hot cities. The spiritual focus of the ensemble at Natanz is the tomb tower of Abu Samad, built in 1307. Though only 19 feet square, this tower is of great aesthetic and emotional power. It is crowned by an octagonal tent dome which in its original state — faced with bright blue tiles — must have appeared in rich contrast to the golden buff of the 123-foot high minaret added in 1324. Broken by shallow bays on each side, the walls thus contain twelve vertical elements all of which lead swiftly upward toward and exciting climax of adroitly composed stalactites that fill the peak of the dome like a sunlit summer cloud.

Light, pouring in through eight windows, is softened by handsome double grilles, shed downwards in a magical but serene glow No direct outside light reaches the worshipper below, only a buoyant radiance. The lower part of the chamber was formerly faced with very fine golden luster tiles focusing on a splendid mihrab.

The adjoining Khaneqah (1316), a monastery or pilgrim's refuge, is completely in ruins except for one of the most beautiful façades in Persia. Much of its exceptional quality is probably due to workmen from the tremendous constructions at Tabriz and Sultaniya. Because of the vigor and variety of its decorative patterns, as well as the intensity and clarity of the turquoise blue facing tiles, the Khaneqah is a fine and instructive example of the period. The portal arch is high and graceful, its spandrels enriched by large disks. Recalling the tomb of Ismail in Bokhara, the façade is a basket-weave pattern instead of the usual floral pattern-arabesques.

The most notable contemporary structure to the east, in Khurasan, is the noble mausoleum at Tus. Imposing by virtue of its size, isolation and compact mass, it is reminiscent of Sultan Sanjar's mausoleum at Merv, especially since in both an external second-story gallery masks the zone of transition. Further comparison with the thirteenth century Jabal-i-Sang at Kirman, more clearly Sasanian in character than the later tombs, sets the development at Tus into perspective. Although much smaller, the structure at Tus also has affinities in its stately proportions with the earlier mausoleum of Uljaitu. Deep vertical channels which impart an appearance of great energy to the façade have their prototypes at Sultaniya. In the environs of the sacred city of Qumm still stand some fifteen tomb towers, all of the fourteenth century. Mostly octagonal, with inward-sloping walls, conical or polyhedral domes and rich interiors, they are decorated with vigorous polychrome and carved ornament. The tomb tower of Imad ad-Din (1390) is a late but fine example of this type. Some stucco ornaments at Qumm closely recall those at Sultaniya, especially in color scheme. There was no royal patronage for these structures, thus, they expressed the standards and tastes of the community, which was high indeed.

The architecture of the Il Khanid Mongols is closely dependent on its antecedents, being in fact a coherent development from previous Seljuk styles and techniques. The relationship between the two styles is so close that in some instances, like the Alaviyan of Hamadan, opinions differ as to whether a building is Seljuk or Mongol. But in general, Mongol architecture had a distinct character of its own, a more colossal scale. Structural components were multiplied and their functions differentiated, solids were diminished, voids increased. Domes, which usually accounted for the upper two-thirds of a structure, were more gracefully united with the buildings they crowned.

Structural problems, more severe than those of Seljuk times, were successfully and ingeniously solved; transverse vaults were perfected (at Yazd and Isfahan) and building with brick was carried to its ultimate triumph (Tomb of Uljaitu, Sultaniya). There was greater emphasis on attenuation and verticality: higher ivans, closely coupled portal minarets, slender colonettes, higher arches, elongated panels. Courts tended to become narrower and the four-ivan plan was perfected. Finally, all the techniques of ornamentation were still further and quite enthusiastically developed.

64

Compared to the finest monuments of the fourteenth century, even the greatest of the earlier buildings (e.g. the Tari-Khana, Gunbad-i-Qabus, the north dome chamber of the Isfahan Jami) were, despite their exceptionally moving powers, somewhat abstract and limited. Splendor and magnificence, legitimate and important in architecture, came in chiefly with the Mongols and their successors, whose buildings generally were saved from mere ostentation by grandeur of scale, harmonious composition and ornamentation that was brilliantly designed and perfectly executed.

VII. REFINEMENT AND OPULENCE

THE TIMURIDS: 1370-1502 A.D.

By 1394, that ferocious warrior, Timur, or Tamerlane, was in the heart of Persia, and the fourteenth century, which began with the rapid creation of beautiful monuments ended in disaster. Timur admired outstanding buildings and systematically collected all kinds of artisans whom he carried off to Samarkand. He rapidly built a series of imposing structures; Registan, the central plaza of Samarkand, became one of the most imposing civic centers ever seen.

Persian architecture of the fourteenth century was based on Seljuk forms and construction, but took on new scale and magnificence. Similarly the architecture of the fifteenth century continued the principals forms of the Mongols, but with greater refinement and consistent skill. Timur, his successors, Shah Rukh, Ulugh Beg, Baysunghur, Abu Said, enthusiastic exponents of Persian culture, presided over a Golden Age which saw all the arts — including the arts of living — carried to new heights of perfection.

Under Timur's imperious driving force, Samarkand, already architecturally rich, once more became "the focus of splendor". "I was determined to built a Masjid-i-Jami in Samarkand which should be without a rival in any country," Timur announced. But, the building was not as imposing as he had expected, so he put the architect to death. Even more ambitious was the conqueror's palace at Kesh, his birthplace. Intended to overawe all who saw it, it was 20 years in building and not quite finished when Clavigo saw it in 1405. The portal arch itself was 165 feet high, flanked by a pair of round towers, like minarets, rising out of a twelve-sided base. The center ivan opened into a huge marble-paved court (300 paces wide). Another great ivan led into a large reception hall tiled with blue and gold, with a ceiling of gold and galleries and numerous chambers to the height of six stories, encrusted with enameled tiles.

No monarch in Asia could boast of anything comparable. A perfect expression of Timur's imperial power and pride, formulated and controlled by Persian aesthetic genius and experience, its gigantic ruins still glow with color, confirming Clavigo's account.

Timur "built more extensively than any other Asian monarch". In order to get a full picture we must supplement the meager appearance of what remains with contemporary written accounts and miniatures: of mural painting, of the marble and porcelain imported from China, of fantastic carvings from India, screens of silver and gold, lavish silk hangings and carpets.

The first, and the greatest surviving, Persian monument of the fifteenth century is the beautiful mosque of Gawhar Shad (1418) now abutting the shrine of the Imam Reza in Mashhad. Its portal continues the Samarkand style of arch within arch, enriched

76

by a succession of bevels and reveals that give it depth and power. The thick, tower-like minarets, merging with the outer corners of the portal screen, extend to the ground and, together with the high foundation revetment of marble, give the ensemble the impression of solidity necessary to support its exuberant color. The entire court façade is faced with enamel brick and mosaic faience of the finest quality. The full scale of colors includes a dominant cobalt blue and turquoise, white, a transparent green, yellow, saffron, aubergine and mirrorblack — all tones fluctuating through several shades. The patterns, lucid and vigorous, are artfully adapted to their decorative role, whether for eye-level panels, or dome ornament meant to be effective at a thousand feet. Monotony, difficult to avoid in such a large area, and a distracting intricacy that might compete with the essential architectural forms are both forestalled. This is accomplished by the energy of the faience floral patterns and brick geometrical schemes; by the emphatic rhythm of the arcades, open galleries and deep recesses; and especially by the striking contrast of the ivans. "It needs no acquaintance with other styles to acclaim this court, among the buildings now existing, as the most beautiful example of color in architecture ever devised". (Robert Byron) The architect was Qavam ad-Din of Shiraz.

Opposite: Gawhar Shad, north-west ivan; below, court, 1418

Gur-i-Mir, Samarkand
detail, faience mosaic panel

One of Timur's most famous buildings, the Gur-i-Mir (1404), his *78* own tomb, is still a monumental and dramatic structure. Externally it is divided into three equal parts. A bulbous dome, 112 feet high, is enriched with 64 almost round flutes and flanked by minarets

Madrassa, Khargird

83 feet high. It is set on a high but narrower cylindrical drum which causes a sharp constriction at the base of the dome. This drum in turn rises out of a chamber which, on the exterior, is octagonal. Portals pierce each of the major four sides, reminiscent of ancient Sasanian practice. The dome is covered with bright blue tiles and the high drum, ornamented with a huge inscription of rectangular Kufic, is of golden-buff bricks — a beautiful contrast characteristic of the fourteenth century. The interior is also impressive, with an alabaster dado, gray-green jasper cornice, black limestone niches, marble balustrade. (In 1454 Ulugh Beg added a superb mosaic faience portal by Mohammad ibnMahmud Isfahani.) *78*

The madrassa at Khargird (completed in 1444-45) is an individual and thoroughly unified building, also designed by Qavam but finished by another Shirazi. It is a carefully proportioned, four-ivan madrassa. The court is square, with ivans of equal height and the portal pavilion of three domed chambers is decorated with painted ornament, delicate carved stucco and intricate stalactites. The tile and mosaic faience of the court are exceptionally forceful in pattern and rich in color. The admirably organized façade, one of the most beautiful in Persia, low and wide, centers on a deep *79* *80*

Madrassa, Khargird,
stucco cornices

portal of modest height; the symmetrical walls to either side of the portal are enriched with pointed arches, inset with rectangular panels and terminate in low corner towers to emphasize horizontality and repose — a new note in Timurid architecture.

Shah Rukh, Timur's son and successor, was responsible for the 80 ambitious musalla and madrassa at Herat, begun in 1417. Shah Rukh was a peace-loving and constructive monarch, who promoted all forms of art and beauty. Qavam ad-Din, a really great architect, an "ornament of the kingdom" was the designer.

Musalla of
Herat

After sketch by E. Durand.

Minaret, Gawhar Shad

Blue Mosque, Tabriz

Further west, Saliha Khanum, the daughter of Jahanshah, was patron of the Blue Mosque of Tabriz (1465). This is one of the few completely roofed mosques of Persia, a necessity in the severe climate of Tabriz. That the dome and minarets have collapsed in this region of severe earthquakes is no reflection on the structural design of the building, which was boldly planned and carefully built. With its new kinds of polychrome ornament, of fresh and beautiful use of color and exquisite workmanship, this building must have been a formidable rival to the mosque of Gawhar Shad.

81

The ornamentation throughout is bold and dramatically varied. As in many mosques, a stout cable molding of intense turquoise frames the portal arch. Inscriptions in gleaming white stand out against dense foliation, all rendered in unparalleled mosaic faience.

The inner sanctuary is faced with huge slabs of Maragha marble bordered with a carved Naskhi inscription, hexagonal tiles of deepest lapis ornamented with gold. Clusters of white stalactites relieve the intense ornamentation. The main dome exterior was covered with white arabesques in relief on a turquoise ground; the smaller dome with white stars, also in relief against a black ground. Pure, intense color, dominantly light blue, has been combined with powerful and original pattern, distributed with imagination and judgement.

The Maydan-i-Shah with . . . Shaykh Lutf Allah . . .

VIII. THE SAFAVID

THE SAFAVIDS:

The Safavid regime was initiated by the dashing Shah Ismail I (1499-1524) who launched his dynasty with a burst of energy. The greatest artists of the day thronged his court, producing many buildings, most of which have been destroyed. The modest Masjid-i-Ali and its decoration fulfilling the most exacting ideals, is the oldest standing Safavid monument, though much restored.

98

Ismail's successor, Shah Tahmasp I, enjoyed a long and uneventful reign (1524-76). His contribution is seen above all in exquisite masterpieces of the decorative arts rather than architecture. His large palace at Qazvin, with its mosaic faience revetments — doubtless of high quality — must have been handsome, but unfortunately it was completely ruined in an earthquake, being constructed of unfired brick. The Masjid-i-Shah in Qazvin, said to be the largest and fairest mosque in Persia, would not withstand the earthquakes that did not even crack the Seljuk dome of the nearby Masjid-i-Jami.

With Shah Abbas I (1589-1627) the great period of Safavid architecture opened, a new period in which the rich, sensationally

. . . Masjid-i-Shah . . . Ali Qapu

CULMINATION

1491-1722 A.D.

colored and imaginative details developed by his predecessors became unified into serene and significant ensembles of immense scale and grandeur. Marked by no great structural innovations, and certainly not Persia's supreme period, it represents the culmination and final expression of Persian Islamic architecture.

Isfahan, designated capital by Shah Abbas I, was reconstituted with so many new mosques, palaces, bridges, avenues and parks that European travelers referred to it as "half the world" and wrote rapturously of its beauty. Chardin, a dependable observer, reports that in 1666 Isfahan had 162 mosques, 48 madrassas, 182 caravanserais and 173 baths. The great maydan at Isfahan, scene of maneuvers, processions and games, especially polo, is surrounded by two-storied arcades which focus on the recessed portal of the Masjid-i-Shah. Opposite, at the north end of the maydan, is the royal caravanserai and bazaar, at the middle of the west side is the palace of Ali Qapu — the seat of government — and facing it, across the maydan, is the private oratory of Shah Abbas, the mosque of Shaykh Lutf Allah.

82-3

The Masjid-i-Shah, begun in 1612, and, despite Shah Abbas' impatience, under construction until 1638, represents the culmination of a thousand years of mosque building in Persia, with a majesty and splendor that places it among the world's greatest buildings. The half-domed arch of the outer portal on the maydan *84* is 90 feet high, the flanking minarets are 130 feet high — with the *85* sanctuary minarets higher still — and the sanctuary dome soaring 163 feet. The recessed portal, almost a building in itself, forms a welcoming embrace, inviting and guiding the throngs outside into *90* the refuge, security and renewal the mosque provides. The two panels which flank the actual entrance within the recess carry the design of a prayer rug, a reminder of the mosque's essential purpose.

←Opposite: Masjid-i-Shah, outer portal; ↑ above, sanctuary portal

At a distance, the imposing mass of this façade, sometimes almost etherealized by its glowing misty blue, quite dominates the maydan and, by contrast with the modest royal palace, proclaims the overwhelming priority of religion over secular power and the central place of religion in the life of the city. 83

This outer portal faces north, as required by the placement of the Maydan, but since the axis of the mosque itself must be in the 89

Masjid-i-Shah, sanctuary

direction of Mecca (hence northeast to southeast), a difficult adjustment was necessary to avoid a sense of dislocation. Through the outer portal one enters a noble vestibule (C on plan), a usual feature. Octagonal, it thus has no particular direction; it can therefore serve as a pivot on which the axis of the building is turned, the gateway to another world of splendor and concentrated power.

84,89

If the glory of the color and the grandeur of the portal screen and dome are almost overwhelming, comprehension is steadied by the rhythmical repetition of the structural elements, symmetrical arcades, balanced ivans, the calm of the wide ablution pool, and the unifying effect of an evenly distributed enveloping color. Over the dome wheel festoons of intricate arabesques in dark blue and golden yellow. The dome, elegant and sensitive in contour, slightly bulbous, set on a high drum, is simple, of remarkably clean and expressive outline uncluttered by any supplementary constructions.

88

— winter prayer hall
— sanctuary portal vault

— vase and shaft motif

— sanctuary dome interior

Both the ground plan and the structure of the building reflect the doctrinal simplicity of Islam. Circulation and communication are everywhere facilitated, nowhere impeded. The common floor level is at no place broken by steps, railings or screens. The walls merge into their garden-like floriation or open onto real and natural gardens. Because of the concentration of the bearing load on octagonal stone columns, wide vistas open up and voids are at maximum. The ornamentation is wholly traditional, repeating

90 92 87

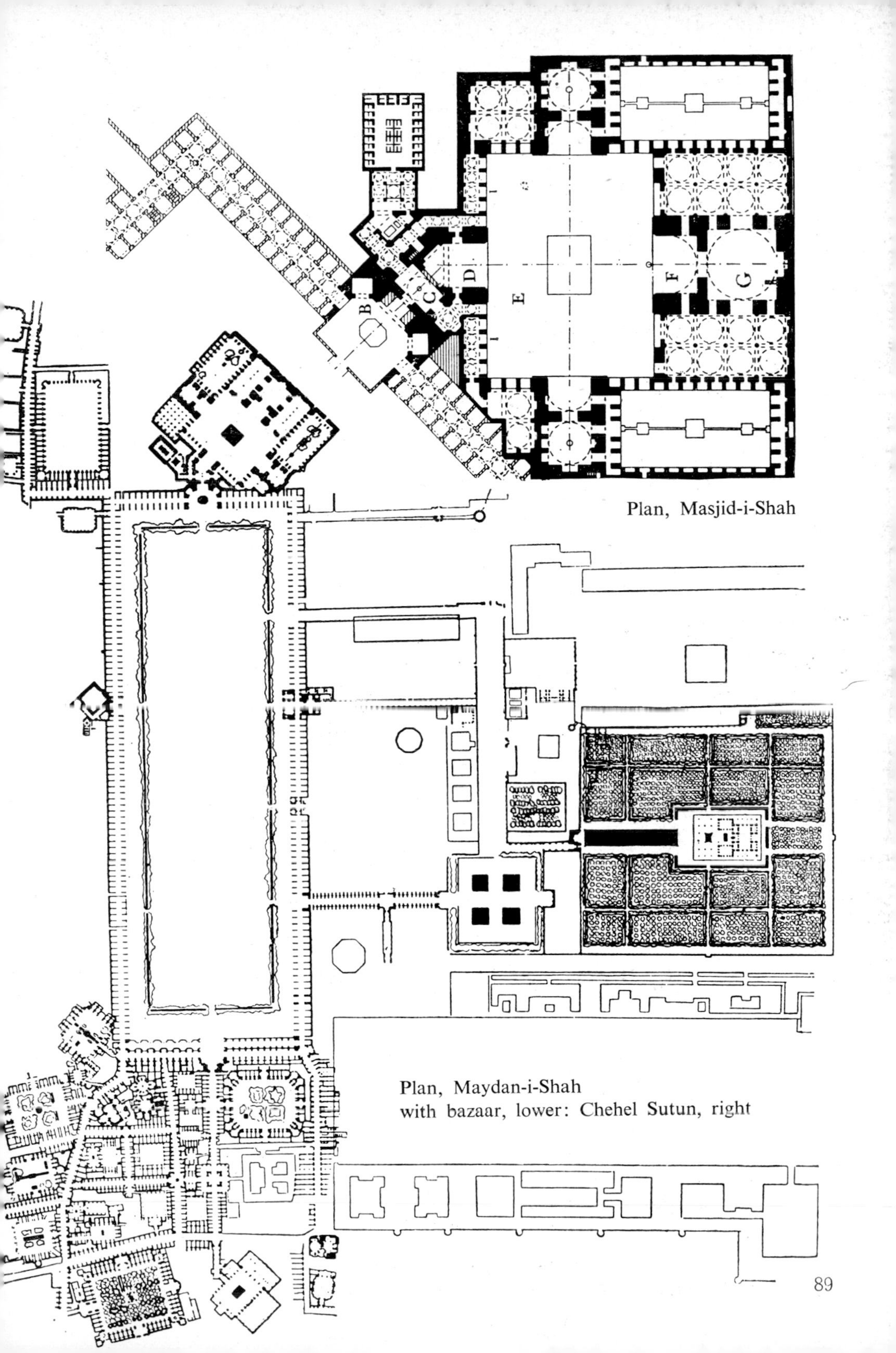

Plan, Masjid-i-Shah

Plan, Maydan-i-Shah
with bazaar, lower: Chehel Sutun, right

Maydan-i-Shah

— mosaic, outer portal

opp.: side dome, interior

— oratory

opp.: window grille

— corridor — looking into inner court

the Iranian motif of appeal for fertility and abundance. Almost the entire surface of the building is covered with enamel tile. A vast display of floral wealth, abstract and imaginative, emphasizes the Persian poetic passion for flowers, as well as the appeal for a continuance of abundant life.

Just as the medieval cathedral expounds pictorially the history and theology of Christianity and by its great forms conveys its mysteries and evokes a moving piety, so also the mosque by its plan and structure declares the Islamic way of life and by its many thousands of inscriptions reports the very word of the prophet. In both, the major structural forms were created by a serious passion for beauty in the conviction that it furnishes in immediate experience, unimpeded by theory or argument, a valid approach to a transcendent reality, the ultimate goal of all worship. In both medieval cathedral and mosque, the deep and lofty vaults, calm and majestic, are eloquent of spiritual certitudes, ultimate verities.

The seventeenth century was not the supreme period of Persian art, and in various details the Masjid-i-Shah is inferior to its model, the mosque of Gawhar Shad, which preceded it by three hundred years. The enamel tile which covers the whole interior of the Masjid-i-Shah is inferior to mosaic faience of preceding centuries or even to its own outer portal. But in nobility, serenity and repose, in powerful affirmation of the spirit of Islam, this building has few rivals.

94
The less ambitious Shaykh Lutf Allah (1601-28) is a contemporary mosque that, because of its modest size and simplified function, is more easily understood. The perennial Sasanian form of a dome on a square chamber, reappears in this beautiful little mosque which Shah Abbas built opposite the palace, in honor of his saintly father-in-law. It is an imposing single chamber, more of a private oratory than a mosque. Here, as in the Masjid-i-Shah, an adjustment was necessary to orient the quibla wall toward Mecca. A diversion of forty-five degrees from the north-south axis of the maydan, effected by an ingenious and inconspicuous turn in the corridor, invisible on the exterior because only the dome appears above the wall that lines the whole maydan.

The low, single-shell dome, 42 feet in diameter, its excessive thrust taken up by massive walls (5 feet, 7 inches thick), gives the building a quiet repose. Midnight blue and white arabesques wheel majestically over a cafe-au-lait color ground, and a brilliant 94 stalactite portal hints at splendor within. The chamber itself marks the final perfection of the dome-on-square plan, now simplified and suave as required by the growing refinement of the period. What was in ground plan just a square, and could have been a monotonous cube, has been developed into a rich and highly dramatic paneled domed octagon, with contrasting treatment of the diagonal and cardinal elements. The abrupt little squinch of Parthian and Sasanian times, so obstructively mechanical, has now been disguised and absorbed. Each corner arch, in reality a gigantic squinch, instead of being a small trumpet-like hollow, now reaches down to the floor. These have the same contour and dimensions as the four main arches, thus transforming the basically square chamber into an octagon. All eight arches are outlined by a thick cable molding of bright turquoise and framed with wide inscription bands of dazzling white on darkest opaque blue, the work of Ali Reza, the greatest calligrapher of the day.

The chamber is entirely empty. Any appurtenances would have been superfluous and quite overwhelmed by the powerful forms and commanding colors. This is pure architecture, flawless and serene, and still as perfect as on the day of dedication three hundred years ago.

Shaykh Lutf Allah — — below, interior of dome

The lighting is a notable feature. The drum of the dome is pierced at regular intervals by windows. These are filled with a pair of grilles, an exterior and an interior grille, each of powerful arabesque patterns in an equal proportion of solids and voids, so that the light is doubly broken and filtered across the edges of cool blue faience. Thus softened and clarified, reflected on innumerable

Shrine of Imam Reza, Mashhad, sanctuary

glittering facets of the wall and dome, light is shed over the shadowless interior like sparkling dew, revealing a perfection of unearthly beauty. No one in a receptive or contemplative mood can enter without a shock and the sense of being received into a Presence. For all its elegance and finish it has no weakness: the scale is too ample, the patterns too strong. Like the inspired architecture it is, it imposes its own mood.

The urge to create perfect ensembles, royal cities, or little "Cities of God," which began in prehistoric times, finds a supreme expression in the sacred shrine of Imam Reza at Mashhad. Here *95* Persia's greatest saint, a presumed martyr to royal jealousy, has long been the focus of piety and intense devotion. For Persians, it

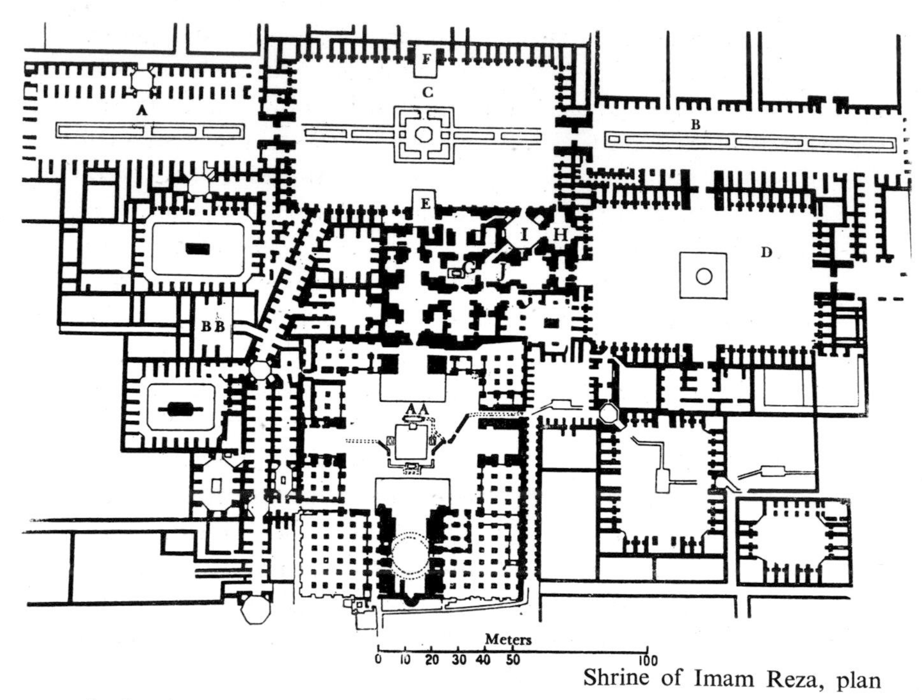

Shrine of Imam Reza, plan

rivals Mecca and on this tomb has been lavished the patronage and wealth of kings and princes. However, since the ninth century it has been ravaged and almost destroyed many times — but reconstructions and additions have occurred even more frequently. Shah Abbas I entered Mashhad in 1597 and ordered restoration in 1601. Without the Safavid contributions, this shrine would not reveal today the concentrated splendor that it does. The holiest site in Persia, and thus difficult to visit for non-religious purposes, it has not yet been thoroughly studied.

It consists of some thirty structures representing more than five centuries of building: mosques, oratories, colleges, libraries, *96* sanctuaries, caravanserais — all connected by four huge courts, from 175 to 350 feet in length, which are surrounded with double-tiered arcades faced with enamel tile. A golden dome and two golden minarets, enriched with white inscriptions on ultramarine bands, are magically reflected in pools. A succession of courts punctuated by portals and twelve high ivans proclaim with dazzling opulence the Shi'ite veneration for the martyred Imam. From the entrance through the upper esplanade, through the old court to the farther end of the lower esplanade (A, C, B on plan) is well over a *77* thousand feet. The fifteenth century mosque of Gawhar (AA), technically separate from the Shrine, is physically contiguous and furnishes an impressive climax to the courts.

The court façades are not everywhere of the highest quality, but the gold ivans are dignified and sumptuous. In their towering masses of softly shining gold framed in glowing blue faience mosaic they are not surpassed for sheer opulence in Islamic architecture. 95

In the old court, facing the gold ivan of Ali Shir Nawai (B on plan), is the blind ivan (F) inscribed as the gift of Shah Abbas II, 1649. Exceedingly tall and narrow, its deep blue-tinted depths make a perfect foil for the golden minaret rising behind it, and its collars of intense ultramarine bearing white inscriptions enhance all. 96

The interior structures are assembled around the sacred tomb chamber of Imam Reza (G), which has been rebuilt and restored many times since the original structure of the ninth century. It is faced with gold- and polychrome luster tiles, some of which date from the thirteenth century. There are special oratories in a variety of styles, from the faience faced Hall of Hospitality (H) with its cascading stalactite vaults, to a nineteenth century mirror-encrusted stalactite dome chamber, the Hall of Mirrors. 97

The most perfect component of the shrine, however, is probably the domed chamber of Allahvardi Khan (I on plan), contemporary with the Shaykh Lutf Allah mosque in Isfahan. An octagonal interior structure, with no façade, the interior walls dissolve

— Imam Reza, Holy of Holies

Masjid-i-Ali, Isfahan — oldest Safavid monument extant

into arches, bays, and galleries, creating the air of a veritable holy of holies. The near blasphemous but almost convincing inscription of the designer proclaims that "this new building that equals in worth the Throne of God is the work of Amir the Architect". Judging by his style, Amir was from Isfahan. The dome of the sanctuary of Allahvardi Khan, 70 feet high and 36 feet in diameter, filled with a mass of stalactites, crowns the two stories of sumptuously modeled recesses, faced with the finest mosaic faience.

Here is space defined, densely compressed; space of expansive force, yet perfectly contained by its harmonious proportions and meticulous organization. Every angle and facet emphasizes location and concentrates on an irresistible marked center which constrains every line of regard and every unconscious movement. One is enclosed in a world of glory that makes the world of common fact seem remote and curiously unreal.

Madrassa Madir-i-Shah, vestibule

Architectural styles, so gradually developed in Persia, were also slow to deteriorate, and their momentum carried them for a while across periods of political and economic decline. Such a decline set in with the death of Shah Abbas I in 1627 when, as Chardin said, "Persia ceased to live". But the madrassa Madir-i-Shah, a mosque and madrassa that Shah Sultan Husayn, the last of the Safavids, built in Isfahan (1706-14) is a noble and handsome building, outshining any comparable contemporary in Islam. *99*

A monumental recessed portal covered with mosaic faience leads from the still beautiful garden boulevard, known as the Chahar Bagh, into a stately garden court. The court façades consist of two-storied open arcades and the four usual vaulted ivans. The

Madir-i-Shah,
sanctuary

100 sanctuary, modeled after the Masjid-i-Shah, has a gracefully con-
109 toured dome. The varied revetments of the building are for the most part of small scale panels created in mingled tonality of gold,
99 green, and shades of blue. This is perhaps the last great building of Iran. Certain later structures, such as the Vakil mosque in Shiraz or the mosque of al-Hakim of Isfahan have charm, but the period of great Persian architecture had already ended.

The Isfahan palaces, of which two have survived, are exceedingly modest in comparison to the royal halls of the Sasanians or

Palace of Chehel Sutun

Mongols. The Chehel Sutun continues the old *talar*, or columnar porch (1647), a form used in palace, temple, mosque and home for centuries. At its simplest it is only a roof-high porch constituting the façade. When attached to a royal building, it provides a huge outdoor reception hall, and is susceptible to lavish embellishments which have included mirror-plated columns, panels and stalactites, and polychrome mosaic ceilings. The interior of this palace is covered with painted ornament of both figurative and abstract designs and capped with ceiling vaults of intense harmonious colors.

101
I, 26
101

— murals

Ali Qapu, interiors

102 The Palace of the Ali Qapu, early 17th century, on the maydan of Isfahan, was the center of government. It is 7 floors tall, square in plan, probably a northern type, with the *talar* as the second story. A huge reception hall capable of holding two hundred or more courtiers, the *talar* commands a fine view over the city with its mosques, domes and minarets, and particularly over the activities in the maydan below. The interior is covered with delicate poly-
102 chrome relief. Many small rooms for private entertainment have fireplaces and are open on one side, evidencing again the Persian technique of bringing the out-of-doors into their houses.

Palace of Ali Qapu

IX. SUMMARY OF FORMS AND STRUCTURAL PROBLEMS

Although the primary task as well as the greatest achievements, of Persian architecture were in the service of religion, architectural activity was by no means confined to religious monuments and secular palaces. Other structures of considerable beauty and requiring equal skill and imagination were built throughout the land. Chief among these were bridges, bazaars, caravanserais, fortifications and gardens, in all but the last case dictated to a certain extent by necessity but given form by aesthetic imagination and practical needs.

THE VAULT, though of less spiritual importance, is absolutely vital to the development of Persia's great architectural achievements. From Sasanian or even late Parthian times, the vault in its various forms was without doubt the most important element in Persian building. Its widespread adoption was necessitated by the lack of sufficient wood and timber to continue the Achaemenid habit of post and lintel construction. Vault construction was already in use from very early times. The Choga Zambil entrance vaults date from about 1200 B.C. *5*

There are three major types of vaults, all derived from a single elemental component: the arch. When an arch is prolonged in *104* depth, a barrel or tunnel vault is created. When two tunnel vaults *104* intersect each other the diagonal vaults thus formed are called cloister or groined vaults. And if the arch is rotated on itself to form an hemispherical vault, it is, of course, a dome. This last, in a more complex form, can become a vault over a square plan and is capable of innumerable variations.

The barrel vault or tunnel vault, the simplest of all, can be built relatively rapidly and cheaply. Such a vault, however, is restricted to a relatively narrow width. Also, since the weight and thrust of such a vault is carried by the walls, they cannot be pierced for windows without seriously, even fatally, weakening the structure; hence the vaults are dark. Despite this, many great structures

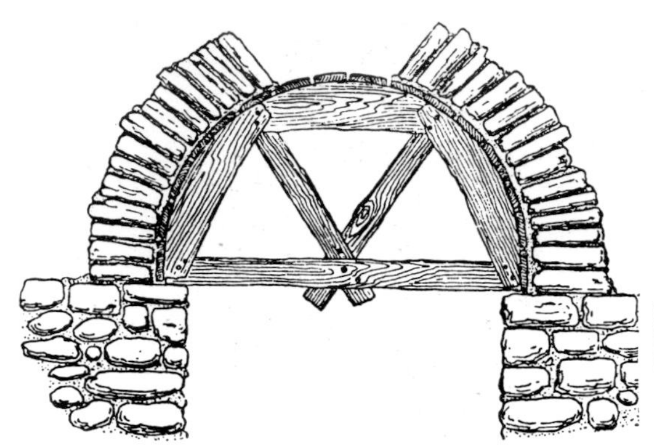

Construction of an arch

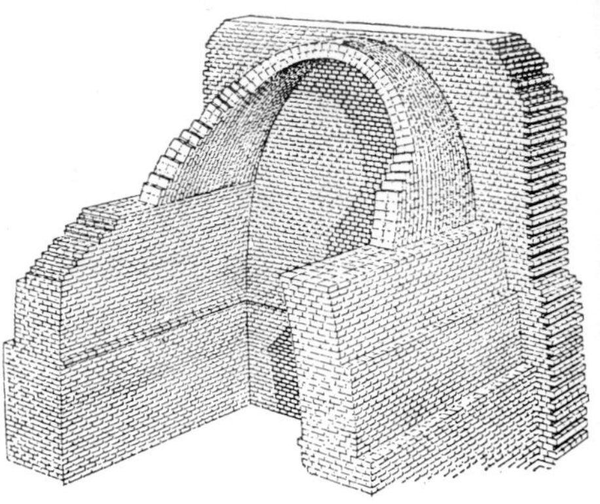

Sasanian barrel vault, cross-section

were built in this form. The single-ivan structure, such as the reception 34 hall of the Taq-i-Kisra, is an example. Generally such vaults are rather monotonous and structurally featureless, except when 32 relieved by arched panels or recessed as at Firuzabad. The problems presented by the barrel vault were in principle solved in Sasanian times by one of the most important inventions in the history of architecture: the transverse arch and vault. The earliest example is the ruined Ivan-i-Kharkha in southwest Persia. These vaults are often very long, as in the great seventeenth century bazaars of Isfahan, Kashan and Shiraz where they extended for hundreds of feet.

With regard to the vault or DOME placed over a square plan, the principal problem is how to manage the transition from square below to circle above. For centuries this problem baffled the very 105 competent Roman engineers, who did not provide an attractive or even assured solution. The earliest solution was reached by Persian engineers and masons who realized that the answer required the development of a third section, a zone of transition between the square chamber below and the round dome above, which involved building an arch across each corner thereby reducing the square to an octagon with a further ring of small arched panels to reduce the eight sides to sixteen, which is close to being a circle.

105 The history of this device; the SQUINCH, is essential to the history of Islamic architecture. The squinches are basically of two types: the hollow round-backed squinch of Sasanian times, and later a simple groined squinch. The problem that immediately followed the initial use of the squinch was how to fill its hollow space. The infinite number of ways in which the squinch is filled, divided or multiplied are astonishing in their variety.

The major question concerns the functional aspects of elements of the vaults, like the INTERSECTING RIBS, for instance. These in Seljuk times are structural as is clearly demonstrated in the Masjid-i-

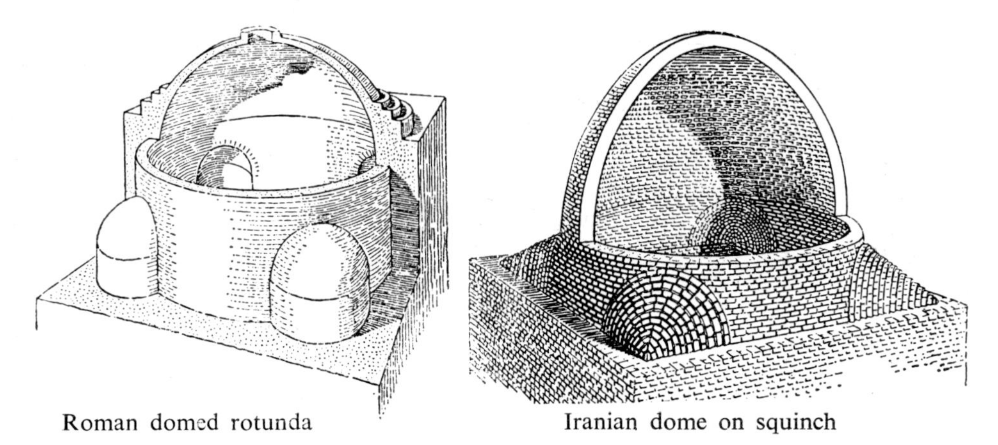

Roman domed rotunda

Iranian dome on squinch

Jami of Isfahan (vaults No. 60—61). Here they carry the weight 53 of the little crowning cupolas. In many other structures down through the 19th century constructive ribs sustain the vault.

Often only the outer line of the ribs, one brick thick, shows; the remainder often composed of a dozen or more bricks are concealed within the shell of the dome, and hence are called 'thief ribs' by the Persian masons. Although today often no longer structural, these lines, by emphasizing the traditional directional energies, create the feeling of active, well co-ordinated and adequate support — all psychological necessities.

Mastery in vault construction was by no means exhausted by the Seljuks or their immediate successors. Its relentless challenge has evoked some surprising creations, such as the vaults in the main caravanserai in Qumm.

An additional type of vault is that built up by STALACTITES. A touch of Persian fancy added to solemn and ponderous structures, they spread throughout the Islamic world. Their charm lay in the multiplication of small but slightly varied units which broke and reflected the light in fascinating patterns.

THE DOME presents many problems and took many forms in Persia. Sasanian domes were round, ovoid, or parabolic. Later they assumed still other shapes: low saucer-like domes that require especially thick walls or buttresses to counter the excessive lateral thrust; or high domes set on tall cylindrical drums as in Timurid times; bulbous domes, expanding much or little beyond the cylindrical base. The onion-shaped dome, a convention of some of the miniature painters, was not beloved by architects because of structural problems involved and its feeling of restlessness, a fault particularly disliked by the Persians. Another type of dome used from the twelfth century was adopted to crown circular or octagonal structures such as tomb towers with a tent or polyhedral roof.

105

78

72

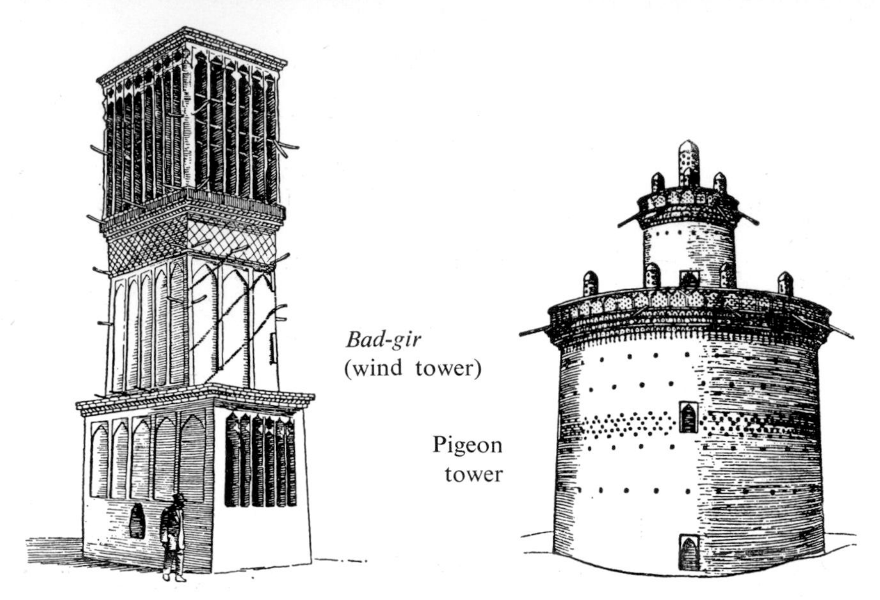

Bad-gir (wind tower)

Pigeon tower

Similarly, less important structures, such as the curious PIGEON 106 TOWERS around Isfahan, originally built to provide fertilizer, are by no means purely functional, but have real grandeur of mass.

Pul-i-Shahristan, Isfahan

BRIDGES, in the southwest, often combined with dams for much needed irrigation, were essential. Bold designing and first-class constructional techniques were indispensable; from Sasanian times they were highly developed. Roman prisoners, including masons captured at Shapur's defeat of Valerian made important contributions: they laid out the mile-long bridge and dam at Shushtar. 106 The remains of the great Pul-i-Dukhtar near Sarvistan, 70 feet high and originally of huge span, confirm the contemporary description of even more sensational structures; the bridge at Idhaj over the 106 Karun river, and the fourteenth century span over the Araxes river near Karkha — built of stone, included one arch 95 feet wide.

Pul-i-Khuda Afarin Araxes river

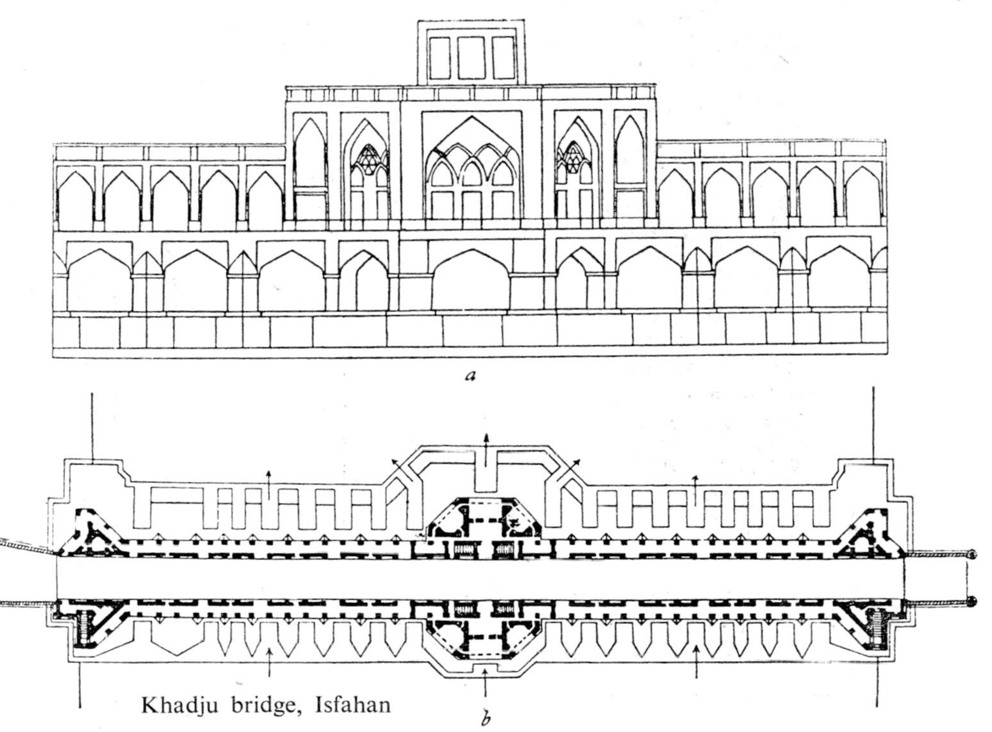

Khadju bridge, Isfahan

These bridges were more than means for crossing a river: they were often of notable beauty in proportions and contour. The later bridges were increasingly elaborate and were sometimes combined with mosques and caravanserais. Thus, two complex bridges over the Zayinda-rud at Isfahan—the bridge of Allahvardi Khan, built by that favorite general of Shah Abbas I, and the Khadju bridge — built by Shah Abbas II, serve both as bridge and dam. Planned also for enjoyment, they are places for tarrying as much as transit. *107*

Walls of Yazd

There were, of course, many other types of public structures, among which is the achievement represented by CITY WALLS. The twelfth to fourteenth century walls of Yazd, which are still standing, are perhaps the most interesting, imposing and skillfully planned. *107*

Qaysariya Bazaar, Isfahan

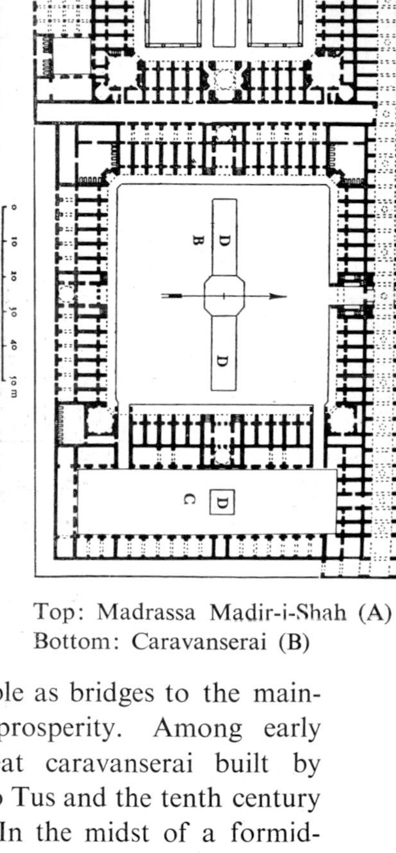

Top: Madrassa Madir-i-Shah (A)
Bottom: Caravanserai (B)

109 CARAVANSERAIS were quite as indispensable as bridges to the maintenance of commercial and economic prosperity. Among early examples of caravanserais are the great caravanserai built by Harun-al-Rashid about 889 on the road to Tus and the tenth century caravanserai built by Adud ad-Dawla. In the midst of a formidable desert, between Samarkand and Bokhara, Sultan Sanjar sometime before 1078 built an immense caravanserai, the magnificent 59 Rabat-i-Malek. At one time in the seventeenth century the caravanserais along the major roads were reputed to be only 20 miles apart, sometimes even closer. They were often quite large and intricate in plan and a famous Seljuk caravanserai at Zabzavar contained 1,700 chambers.

These caravanserais constitute one of the triumphs of Persian architecture. Nowhere can we find a more complete accord of function and structure. The basic plan for later caravanserais is constant from structure to structure. All are essentially concentric, 108 with the outer wall quite blank, allowing access only through a single and easily defended portal. The central court is surrounded by open

Madrassa Madir-i-Shah, seen from its caravanserai, now —
The Shah Abbas Hotel, Isfahan

arcades, like a mosque or madrassa, the middle of each side sometimes being emphasized by a larger arch or even a vault — in effect the conventional four-ivan plan. All the requirements for defense and service, the primary considerations of these structures, are fully met. The amenities were not neglected either. The outer walls were frequently faced with enameled tiles and the portals occasionally rival even the great mosque portals. *109*

The system of the caravanserais logically leads to . . .

BAZAARS, those centers of commercial and civic activity. The standard plan, called the *chahar-su* (four rivers), consisted of two passageways intersecting each other at right angles, covered by a dome at the crossing. Small apertures in the vaulted roof let in sufficient light yet kept out the intense heat of summer and retained warmth in winter. Here, public opinion was made and expressed and social intercourse flourished. The handsomest bazaar of all was the Qaysariya of Isfahan, built by Shah Abbas I at the beginning of the seventeenth century. *108* *108*

Ghavam House, Shiraz, mirror salon —painted ceiling
—porch

PERSIAN DOMESTIC ARCHITECTURE is, in many periods, quite worthy of note. Every house of at least middle-class status has its own pool. For protection, most have traditionally had an off-axis entrance (as did the caravanserais). The intense heat of the summer is allayed in a variety of ways and with skill: indoor as well as out- *111* door pools, open water channels running through the house, sub- *106* basement chambers aerated by the handsome *bad-girs* (wind towers).

Ghavam House, central courtyard

Persian gardens, in contrast to these decorative structures, which also filled every specific and necessary function, served more psychic and less measurable needs. In the prehistoric Samarra pottery we find the typical garden lay-out, based on the *chahar-su*; the crossing of two canals with birds and trees in each of the four corners. Cyrus the Great told Lysander that he had himself planned the great park at Sardis and had planted trees with his own hands. The gardens of the Achaemenid empire were carefully designed with rectangles, alleys and symmetrical trees. By the time of the Sasanian empire, gardens were of vast extent and parks might cover ten square miles. One example was the garden of the Imarat-i-Khusraw, the fabulous palace built by Chosroes II. In Islamic times huge gardens were symmetrically laid out in relation to the main axis of the building.

Basement, *zir-zamin*, Moghadam House, Tehran

The Narenjestan: above, main building; opposite, garden plan

The terminal points were marked by pavilions. The palace was located at the intersection of two avenues and water courses at right angles to the main axis thus provided long vistas framed by parallel water channels. The whole area was further divided into rectangular beds defined by small water channels. The walled garden had, from Achaemenid times, been called *Paradaiza*, and paradise it was, and the garden ideal penetrated nearly all the arts.

THE PATRONS' ambitions, hopes and sometimes quite specific prescriptions were generally the immediate creative force behind the finest achievements of Persian architecture. This decisive influence under the Achaemenids was constantly renewed in later periods.

The immense programs of the Ghaznavids, especially under Mahmud's personal impetus, have been established by contemporary documents and existing ruins. If anything, however, the importance of architecture grew successively under the Seljuks, especially Nizam-al-Mulk, and the Mongols, Ghazan Khan, Uljaitu, and Ali Shah, until it became obsessive under the Timurids.

The execution of the often extravagant visions of these monarchs and patrons was the work of professionals, about whose training and operations we know all too little.

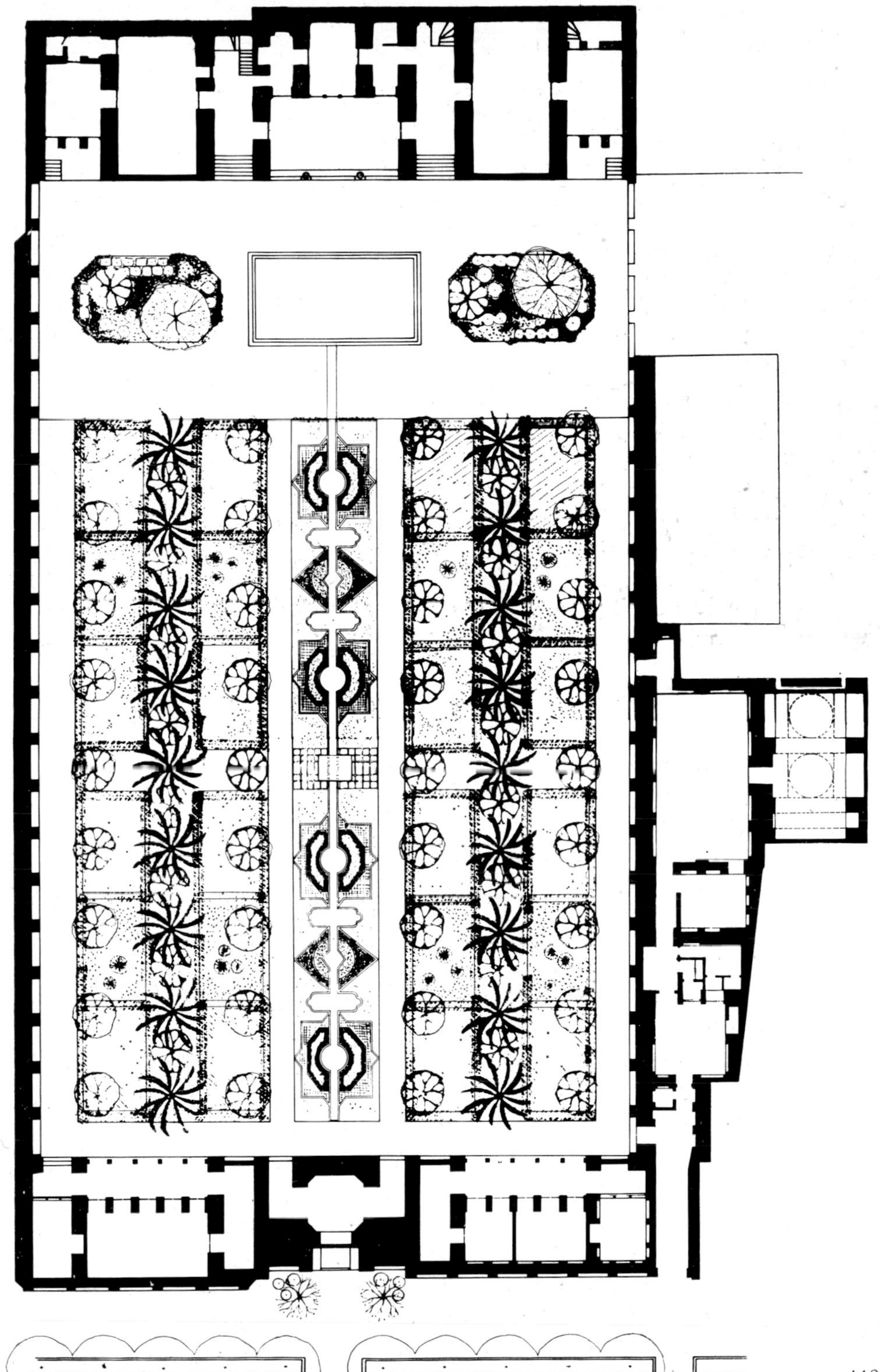

Conclusion

The architecture of Persia across the centuries displays great variety, both structural and aesthetic, developing gradually and coherently out of prior traditions and experience. Without sudden innovations, and despite the repeated trauma of invasions and cultural shocks, it has achieved an individuality distinct from that of other Muslim countries. Its paramount virtues are several: a marked feeling for form and scale; structural inventiveness, especially in vault and dome construction; a genius for decoration with a freedom and success not rivaled in any other architecture.

While plan and layout, especially in later centuries, was of the highest order, construction was rarely equal in solidity and sophistication to European masonry. But the very survival of so many early monuments — especially the lofty minarets — in a country afflicted by devastating invasions and earthquakes, to say nothing of the damage inflicted by brick-hungry villagers, is proof that permanence was an effective ideal for many architects. With the exception of the costly mosaic faience, the materials used in Persian building and the methods employed permitted rapid and inexpensive construction, so that a relatively small country was able to create a disproportionately large number of important monuments.

There was a *humane* character to all the arts of Persia. This humanity is evident in the architecture, which in the Islamic period, especially, was for the general benefit, accessible and shared by all.

The continuity of Persian Architecture was nearly severed in the 18th century. The brutal invasion of the Afghans, the costly and futile wars of Nader Shah, and the cultural crudity of the Qajar dynasty succeeding the economic depression due to loss of European markets, were all hostile to the noble and refined spirit of Persian Architecture.

But the tradition was too deep to be wholly extinguished, and, in addition to the powerful forms of the citadel walls of Karim Khan, a good bazaar and mosque in Shiraz, there was a masterpiece in plain white of intersecting arches and stalactites in the caravanserai at Qumm, and a very beautiful sanctuary, of simple but strong and sensitive form, in the Masjid-i-Jami in Tabas.

Doshan Tepe, Kiosk in Qasr-i-Qajar, Tehran

The palaces of the Qajars in the nineteenth century were mostly hastily built and of dubious taste. But the Qajar pavilion at 115 Doshan Tepe, Tehran, has dignity and charm, and three palaces in Shiraz are well built: the Bagh-i-Eram and the Narenjestan have 112 vigorous and forcefully expressed façades, while the house of 111 Ghavam has a large court of simple beauty and gorgeous interior, largely made of tiny fragments of mirror glass — like the Hall of 110 Mirrors at Mashhad, but even more brilliant. The Narenjestan was the reception hall and the adjoining palace, the living quarters. The Narenjestan is now occupied by the Asia Institute of Pahlavi University while the Bagh-i-Eram is the residence and reception back cover hall of the Chancellor of Pahlavi University.

But if Persian Architecture in part survived the vicissitudes of the eighteenth and nineteenth centuries, it is not certain that it has survived the impact of European styles. All this came at a time when Iran — forgetting her own past, was particularly vulnerable to novelty and propaganda. Many substantial monuments have been built and suggested without any hint of the immensely rich and vital architectural tradition of Persia, in the so-called International style, that might quite as well have been built in Oregon, Uruguay, Finland, New Zealand or Japan — as if Persian architectural tradition had been played out after 3000 years of continuous evolution, with an imposing record of masterpieces: Persepolis, Sarvistan, Gunbad-i-Qabus, the Mausoleum of Uljaitu, the Madrassa of Khargird, the Mosque of Gawhar Shad, the Blue Mosque of Tabriz, the Masjid-i-Shah and the Shaykh Lutf Allah of Isfahan — all holding their own with the finest architecture the world has seen, all different, yet, all Persian.

Index

numerals indicate page: light-face = text, *italic* = illustration, **bold** = color plate

LIBRARY OF INTRODUCTIONS TO PERSIAN ART

in English, Persian and other Language Editions

*Arthur Upham Pope — *Introducing* PERSIAN ARCHITECTURE

Arthur Upham Pope — *Introducing* PERSIAN ARCHITECTURAL DECORATION

Phyllis Ackerman — *Introducing* PERSIAN TEXTILES

*Werner Felix Dutz — *Introducing* PERSEPOLIS AND THE ARCHAEOLOGICAL SITES OF FARS

also in German Edition

Ali Hakemi — *Introducing* KALURAZ

Ezat O. Negahban — *Introducing* MARLIK, CITY OF THE MIGHTY MEDES

Robert Dyson — *Introducing* HASANLU, CITY OF THE GOLDEN BOWL

Steve Evans — *Introducing* PERSIAN GARDENS

Ralph Pinder-Wilson — *Introducing* PERSIAN AND ISLAMIC GLASS

Andrew Williams — *Introducing* PERSIAN CERAMICS

Arthur Upham Pope, Eric Schroeder and Jay Gluck — *Introducing* ISFAHAN, CITY OF HALF THE WORLD

Jay and Sumi Gluck — *Introducing* PERSIAN FOLK ARTS

*Already published

Published through assistance of
The Harry Gluck Memorial Rotating Publication Fund

Text set and printed by Kokusai Insatsu, Osaka
Photo plates by Hanshichi Shashin Insatsu, Tokyo
Color plates and printing by Hanshichi Shashin Insatsu
Bound at Kokusai Insatsu, Osaka